Disputed Questions on Papal Infallibility

Disputed Questions
on
Papal Infallibility

by John P. Joy

S JUSTI
PRESS

Lincoln, Nebraska

Os Justi Press
Lincoln, NE
https://osjustipress.com/

Inquiries to
professorkwasniewski@gmail.com

ISBN 9798360217930

Contents

Part I
Disputed Questions on Papal Infallibility

QUESTION I
On the Extension and Limits of Papal Infallibility

Question II

On Particular Cases of Papal Teaching

Part II
Essays on Papal Authority

Preface

The First Vatican Council solemnly defined that the pope is infallible when he speaks *ex cathedra*, that is, from the chair of St. Peter, which is the chair of truth:

> Therefore, faithfully adhering to the tradition received from the beginning of the Christian faith, for the glory of God our Savior, for the exaltation of the Catholic religion, and for the salvation of Christian peoples, with the approval of the sacred council, We teach and define that it is a divinely revealed dogma: that the Roman Pontiff, when he speaks *ex cathedra*, that is, when, exercising his office as shepherd and teacher of all Christians, in virtue of his supreme apostolic authority, he defines a doctrine concerning faith or morals to be held by the whole Church, possesses, by the divine assistance promised to him in blessed Peter, that infallibility with which the divine Redeemer willed his Church to be endowed in defining doctrine concerning faith or morals; and therefore, that such definitions of the Roman Pontiff are irreformable of themselves, and not by the consent of the Church. But if anyone, which God forbid, should presume to contradict this Our definition: let him be anathema.[1]

---

[1]   First Vatican Council, Dogmatic Constitution on the Church of Christ, *Pastor Aeternus* (1870), ch. 4 (translation mine).

With this definition, the question as to whether the pope is able to speak infallibly at all has been finally settled; since then, theological discussion has centered on the subsidiary questions as to how often and under what conditions he does so.

There are two errors to be avoided here. On the one hand, we must avoid the very real phenomenon of "creeping infallibilization,"[2] according to which almost every utterance of the pope is regarded as being (at least practically) infallible. On the other hand, we must be wary of the equally dangerous tendency to interpret the conditions for papal infallibility so restrictively as to render the dogma almost meaningless. Paradoxically, these opposite tendencies seem to be almost equally widespread among Catholics in general. One constantly encounters the idea that the pope has spoken infallibly only twice—that is, in defining the dogmas of the Immaculate Conception and Assumption of Mary—and yet, it is also everywhere assumed (indeed, often by the same people!) that no pope could possibly teach anything false in any of his official teaching on faith or morals. As is so often the case, the truth lies in between.

There are many questions involved here that need to be untangled, and so I have chosen the format of the medieval scholastic disputation in an effort to bring some measure of greater clarity to the topic. There are two main questions to be considered concerning the infallibility of the pope: the first concerns the extension and limits of papal infallibility in general; the second concerns

---

[2] See Wolfgang Beinert, "Unfehlbarkeit," in *Lexicon für Theologie und Kirche*, 3rd ed., ed. Walter Kasper, vol. 10 (Freiburg im Breisgau: Herder, 1993–2001), 390. See also Augustin Schmied, "'Schleichende Infallibilisierung': Zur Diskussion um das kirchliche Lehramt," in *In Christus zum Leben befreit: Festschrift für Bernhard Häring*, ed. Josef Römelt and Bruno Hidber (Freiburg: Herder, 1992), 250–72.

particular cases of papal teaching. These questions constitute Part I of the present book. Question I was first published in *Nova et Vetera* [English ed.] 19.1 (2021): 33–61.

Part II consists of several essays that further explicate topics treated scholastically in Part I. These essays were first published at *OnePeterFive* and *The Josias*. I am grateful to their editors for permission to include them in this volume.

The appendix presents an essay by Dr. Jeremy Holmes, Associate Professor of Theology at Wyoming Catholic College, an earlier version of which appeared at *Catholic World Report* on December 30, 2017. It fills in a key piece of the picture: Why are there are such different levels in the magisterium to begin with? Why shouldn't all papal or conciliar teaching be infallible? What is it about the nature of authority itself that suggests we should expect both infallible *and* fallible teaching, both definitive and non-definitive exercises of authority? Dr. Holmes brings to the question his usual penetrating philosophical insight, and we are grateful to him for allowing us to include his essay.

The current Dicastery for the Doctrine of the Faith was, prior to Pentecost of 2022, called the Congregation for the Doctrine of the Faith (=CDF). Since these pages frequently refer to documents published by an entity then known as the CDF, this manner of reference has been retained.

John P. Joy

October 11, 2022

Feast of the Divine Maternity

PART I

Disputed Questions on
Papal Infallibility

On the Extension and Limits of Papal Infallibility

Concerning this first question, there are seven points to be considered: (1) whether the essential conditions for speaking *ex cathedra* are rightly enumerated as three; (2) whether the pope is able to teach any error at all in the exercise of his authentic magisterium; (3) whether the infallibility of the pope is limited to the exercise of his extraordinary magisterium; (4) whether the pope is able to speak infallibly when he confirms or reaffirms a doctrine already infallibly taught by the ordinary and universal magisterium; (5) whether the infallibility of the pope is limited to defining dogmas of divine and Catholic faith; (6) whether the infallibility of the pope extends to the canonization of saints; (7) whether the pope is able to speak infallibly without explicitly addressing the universal Church.

ARTICLE 1

Whether the Essential Conditions for Speaking *Ex Cathedra* Are Rightly Enumerated as Three?

OBJECTION 1. It seems that the essential conditions for speaking *ex cathedra* are not rightly enumerated as three. For Saint John Henry Newman enumerates four conditions, saying: "He speaks *ex cathedra*, or infallibly, when he speaks, first, as the Universal

Teacher; secondly, in the name and with the authority of the Apostles; thirdly, on a point of faith or morals; fourthly, with the purpose of binding every member of the Church to accept and believe his decision."[3]

OBJECTION 2. Furthermore, Monsignor Joseph Clifford Fenton enumerates five conditions, saying that the pope is infallible when: "A) He speaks in his capacity as the ruler and teacher of all Christians. B) He uses his supreme apostolic authority. C) The doctrine on which he is speaking has to do with faith or morals. D) He issues a certain and definitive judgment on that teaching. E) He wills that this definitive judgment be accepted as such by the universal Church."[4]

OBJECTION 3. Furthermore, even if there are only three conditions given in the body of the definition of papal infallibility, we must add another condition, which is that the pope must be faithfully interpreting divine revelation and not inventing any new doctrine. For the First Vatican Council teaches that "the Holy Spirit was promised to the successors of Peter not so that they might, by his revelation, make known some new doctrine, but that, by his assistance, they might religiously guard and faithfully expound the revelation or deposit of faith transmitted by the apostles."[5] The Second Vatican Council also teaches that, "when

---

[3] John Henry Newman, *A Letter Addressed to His Grace the Duke of Norfolk on Occasion of Mr. Gladstone's Recent Expostulation* (London: Pickering, 1875), 115; see also Joachim Salaverri, *Tractatus de Ecclesia Christi* (Madrid: Biblioteca de Autores Cristianos, 1955), no. 594.

[4] Joseph C. Fenton, "Infallibility in the Encyclicals," *American Ecclesiastical Review* 128 (1953): 177–98, at 186.

[5] Vatican I, *Pastor Aeternus*, ch. 4 (*Documents of Church Councils*, ed. Norman P. Tanner, 2 vols. [Washington, DC: Georgetown University Press, 1990], 2:816).

either the Roman Pontiff or the body of bishops together with him defines a judgment, they pronounce it in accordance with revelation itself, which all are obliged to abide by and be in conformity with."[6] And again: "The Roman Pontiff and the bishops, in view of their office and the importance of the matter, by fitting means diligently strive to inquire properly into that revelation and to give apt expression to its contents; but a new public revelation they do not accept as pertaining to the divine deposit of faith."[7]

ON THE CONTRARY, Bishop Vincent Ferrer Gasser, in his official *relatio* delivered at the First Vatican Council in order to explain the intended sense of the definition of papal infallibility, enumerates three essential conditions that restrict the infallibility of the pope: "The infallibility of the Roman Pontiff is restricted by reason of the *subject*, that is when the pope, constituted in the chair of Peter, the center of the Church, speaks as universal teacher and supreme judge: it is restricted by reason of the *object*, i.e., when treating of matters of faith and morals; and by reason of the *act itself*, i.e., when the pope defines what must be believed or rejected by all the faithful."[8]

I ANSWER THAT it must be said that the pope speaks *ex cathedra*, and hence infallibly, whenever three essential conditions are fulfilled, and these pertain to the subject, the object, and the

---

6 Second Vatican Council, Dogmatic Constitution on the Church, *Lumen Gentium* (1964), §25.

7 Vatican II, *Lumen Gentium*, §25.

8 Vincent Ferrer Gasser, *The Gift of Infallibility: The Official* Relatio *on Infallibility of Bishop Vincent Ferrer Gasser at Vatican Council I*, trans. James T. O'Connor, 2nd ed. (San Francisco: Ignatius Press, 2008), 49. Italics are in the original Latin text (*Sacrorum Conciliorum Nova et Amplissima Collectio* [hereafter, "Mansi"], ed. J. D. Mansi, vol. 52 [Florence, 1759; repr. Paris: H. Welter, 1901–1927], 1214 C).

act of the teaching. This is evident both from Gasser's *relatio* at the First Vatican Council and from the Second Vatican Council's reformulation of the doctrine, according to which: "The Roman Pontiff, the head of the college of bishops, in virtue of his office, enjoys this infallibility when, [subject:] as supreme shepherd and teacher of all Christ's faithful, who confirms his brethren in their faith (Lk 22:32), [act:] he proclaims by a definitive act, [object:] a doctrine concerning faith or morals."[9]

REPLY TO OBJECTION 1. To the first it must be said that the first two conditions enumerated by Cardinal Newman are really only one, for the pope does not speak as universal shepherd and teacher otherwise than in virtue of his supreme apostolic authority. This can be seen in the reformulation of the teaching in *Lumen Gentium* §25, which places the phrase "in virtue of his office" prior to and outside of the enumeration of conditions contained in the *cum* ("when") clause: that is, the pope is infallible, *when* ... etc.

REPLY TO OBJECTION 2. To the second it must be said that the first two conditions enumerated by Fenton are really only one in the same way as those enumerated by Newman; and the last two conditions enumerated by Fenton are likewise only one: for whenever the pope as supreme head of the Church issues a definitive judgment on a matter of faith or morals, then it follows as a necessary consequence that this judgment must be accepted as such by the universal Church. This too can be seen in the re-formulation of the teaching in *Lumen Gentium* §25, which does not include the phrase "to be held by the whole Church" within the clause where the conditions for infallibility are enumerated.

REPLY TO OBJECTION 3. To the third it must be said that this argument reduces the dogma of papal infallibility to a meaningless

---

9 Vatican II, *Lumen Gentium*, §25.

tautology. For it amounts to saying that the pope is infallible whenever he speaks the truth, which is the same as saying that he always speaks truly when he speaks truly. But absolutely everyone is infallible in this sense. It should rather be understood that this "requirement" for the pope to speak in accordance with divine revelation when he defines a doctrine is not given as a *condition* by which to judge whether the pope has spoken infallibly, but as an *assurance* that when he does speak infallibly, what he says will in fact be in accordance with divine revelation. This is why both *Pastor Aeternus* and *Lumen Gentium* place this teaching outside the enumeration of conditions for papal infallibility. Hence we should not say that, if the pope acting as supreme head of the Church were to define by a solemn judgment that there are four persons in the holy Trinity, he would not in that case have fulfilled the conditions for speaking infallibly, and hence that he could have taught, and in fact did teach, error. Rather we must say that, because the pope is infallible when he defines a matter of faith or morals by a solemn judgment, God will therefore prevent him from promulgating such a definition. In other words, the dogma of papal infallibility does not *account for*, but rather *rules out*, this hypothetical possibility.

As for how God prevents the pope from solemnly defining a false doctrine, this could be by an external act of providence, by which God would cause the pope to lose his voice or his pen or even his life in order to prevent him from promulgating an erroneous definition; but we ought rather to believe that God ordinarily accomplishes this by the internal working of grace, by which would move the pope to change his mind about a false doctrine he had intended to define. For this is more consistent with the ordinary working of divine providence, which "reaches from end to end mightily, and orders all things sweetly" (Wis 8:1).

ARTICLE 2

Whether the Pope Is Able to Teach Any Error at All in the Exercise of His Authentic Magisterium?

OBJECTION 1. It seems that the pope is not able to teach any error at all in the exercise of his authentic magisterium. For according to Joachim Salaverri, what is taught by the authentic magisterium of the pope is taught by the Church.[10] And according to the Roman Catechism, "This one Church cannot err in faith or morals, since it is guided by the Holy Ghost."[11] Likewise, the Baltimore Catechism says: "The Church cannot err when it teaches a doctrine of faith or morals."[12]

OBJECTION 2. Furthermore, according to Pope John Paul II: "Alongside this infallibility of *ex cathedra* definitions, there is the charism of the Holy Spirit's assistance, granted to Peter and his successors so that they would not err in matters of faith and morals, but rather shed great light on the Christian people. This charism is not limited to exceptional cases, but embraces in varying degrees the whole exercise of the magisterium."[13] Therefore, etc.[14]

---

[10] Salaverri, *Tractatus de Ecclesia Christi*, nos. 657–60; see also no. 892.

[11] *Catechism of the Council of Trent* (1566), trans. John McHugh and Charles Callan (Rockford, IL: TAN Books, 1982), I, a. 9.

[12] *Baltimore Catechism* (1891), no. 526 (http://www.baltimore-catechism.com/lesson12.htm).

[13] Pope John Paul II, General Audience of March 24, 1993, §4 (English trans. from "The Holy Spirit Assists the Roman Pontiff," totus2us.com/teaching/jpii-catechesis-on-the-church/the-holy-spirit-assists-the-roman-pontiff/).

[14] Stephen Walford makes this argument in "The Magisterium of Pope Francis: His Predecessors Come to His Defense," *Vatican Insider*, February 7, 2017, lastampa.it/Vatican-insider/en/2017/02

OBJECTION 3. Furthermore, according to the Second Vatican Council, the faithful are required to accept the teaching of the authentic papal magisterium with a "religious submission of will and intellect."[15] If, therefore, the pope were able to teach error in the exercise of his authentic magisterium, Catholics could be required to accept something that is false, which would be opposed to the indefectibility of the Church. Therefore, etc.

OBJECTION 4. Furthermore, the pope is the final judge in matters of faith and morals. Hence, there can be no legitimate dissent from any papal teaching nor appeal to any other authority. But this would place the faithful in an impossible situation if the pope were at all able to teach error.

OBJECTION 5. Furthermore, according to Gasser's *relatio* on papal infallibility, the First Vatican Council raised to a dogma the teaching of Saint Robert Bellarmine regarding the extent of papal infallibility.[16] But Cardinal Bellarmine held it to be a pious and probable opinion "that the Sovereign Pontiff not only cannot err as Pontiff, but also that as a particular person he cannot be a heretic, by obstinately believing something false contrary to the faith."[17] Therefore, it is now a dogma of faith that the pope is in no way able to teach error in matters of faith or morals.[18]

/07/news/the-magisterium-of-pope-francis-his-predecessors-come-to-his-defense-1.34649513.

[15] Vatican II, *Lumen Gentium*, §25.

[16] Gasser, *Gift of Infallibility*, 59.

[17] Robert Bellarmine, *Controversies of the Christian Faith*, trans. Kenneth Baker (Saddle River, NJ: Keep the Faith, 2016), 970.

[18] Emmett O'Regan makes this argument in "The Heretical Pope Fallacy: The Official *Relatio* of Vatican I on the Dogmatization of St. Bellarmine's 'Fourth Opinion,'" *Vatican Insider*, December 11, 2017, lastampa.it/Vatican-insider/en/2017/12/11/news/the-heretical-pope-fallacy-1.34082024.

OBJECTION 6. Furthermore, according to the Congregation for the Doctrine of the Faith (CDF), propositions contrary to the non-definitive teaching of the authentic magisterium "can be qualified as *false* or, in the case of teachings of the prudential order, as rash or dangerous and therefore *tuto doceri non potest*."[19] But if all speculative propositions contrary to the teaching of the authentic magisterium are false, then all such propositions taught by the authentic magisterium must be true.

OBJECTION 7. Furthermore, according to Cardinal Johann Baptist Franzelin, in addition to the gift of "infallible truth," which protects the *ex cathedra* definitions of the pope, there is also the gift of "infallible security," which guarantees that all authentic papal teaching, even if not infallibly *true*, is at least infallibly *safe*, so that it would always be safe for the faithful to embrace it and it could never be safe to reject it.[20] Therefore, the authentic magisterium of the pope is at least practically infallible.

OBJECTION 8. Furthermore, according to Cardinal Louis Billot, the non-definitive exercise of the authentic magisterium consists in probabilistic rather than in certain judgments. Thus, when the pope teaches a doctrine of faith or morals without intending to proclaim it definitively, he is to be understood as proposing that this doctrine is *probably* true (and therefore *safe* to hold) in light of current knowledge. Such teaching is "reformable" in the sense that the Church, enlightened by new knowledge, could later teach that the reverse is true. And yet this would not make the previous

---

[19] Congregation for the Doctrine of the Faith (CDF), *Doctrinal Commentary on the Concluding Formula of the Profession of Faith* (1998), §10.

[20] See Johann Baptist Franzelin, *Tractatus de divina traditione et scriptura* (Rome: Marietti, 1870), 116.

teaching false, since it was rightly considered probable at the time. Therefore, even the reformable teaching of the pope cannot be said to be in error. As Billot says: "That which is not safe now, looking at the present state of the question, can later become safe, when new evidence has appeared: and thus the decision declaring as safe that which was said before not to be safe, would not strictly speaking be a reformation of the sentence, but a new declaration not contrary to the prior one."[21]

ON THE CONTRARY, according to Pope John Paul II, "The non-infallible expressions of the authentic magisterium of the Church should be received with religious submission of mind and will."[22] But if there are non-infallible expressions of the authentic magisterium, then it is possible for the authentic magisterium to teach error. For what is not infallible is fallible; and what is fallible is able to fail.

I ANSWER THAT, it must be said that it is possible for the pope to teach error in the exercise of his authentic magisterium, although the divine assistance granted to him in virtue of his supreme office prevents this from occurring frequently. The charism of infallibility is bestowed on the Church by God in order to protect the faithful from being forced by holy obedience into error in matters of faith or morals. Since the solemn judgments or definitions of the pope are strictly binding in conscience, if the pope were able to err in such judgments, then all Christ's faithful could be obliged to believe something against the Faith, which would be contrary to the indefectibility of the Church,

---

[21] Louis Billot, *Tractatus de Ecclesia Christi*, q. 10, th. 19, in vol. 1, 3rd ed. (Rome: Giachetti, 1909), 437.

[22] Pope John Paul II, Address to the Bishops from the United States of America on Their *Ad Limina* Visit, October 15, 1988, §5.

according to the words of Christ, "The gates of hell shall not prevail against it" (Matt 16:18). But when the pope teaches a matter of faith or morals in his authentic magisterium without speaking *ex cathedra*, then he does not require a definitive assent from the faithful. Hence, if he should err in such teaching, the whole Church would not necessarily be led astray by the error. Therefore, it is not necessary that this kind of teaching should be absolutely protected from all error. Yet it is more fitting that even this kind of teaching should be protected from frequent error, lest anyone be led to conclude that the Church "does not enjoy divine assistance in the integral exercise of its mission."[23]

Moreover, according to the Second Vatican Council, the response owed by the faithful to the authentic magisterium of the pope when he is not speaking *ex cathedra* is a "religious submission of will and intellect."[24] According to the official notes provided by the Theological Commission at Vatican II, this text is intended to be understood in reference to *non-infallible* teaching. One note mentions that this clause was added "in order to determine further what assent ought to be given to the teaching of the authentic magisterium *below the grade of infallibility*."[25] When the text was later relocated, there is another note that "it seemed better to treat of the *non-infallible* magisterium of the Roman pontiff in the context of the magisterium of the whole episcopal body."[26] Thus it is clear that, according to the intended sense of *Lumen*

---

[23] CDF, Instruction on the Ecclesial Vocation of the Theologian, *Donum Veritatis* (1990), §24.

[24] Vatican II, *Lumen Gentium*, §25.

[25] *Acta Synodalia Sacrosancti Concilii Oecumenici Vaticani Secundi* (Rome: Typis Polyglottis Vaticanis, 1970–1999), 2/1:255 (emphasis added).

[26] *Acta Synodalia* 3/1:250 (emphasis added).

Gentium §25, the authentic magisterium of the pope is not always infallible, which means that it may sometimes teach error.

The religious submission of will and intellect that is normally due to the teaching of the authentic magisterium is a genuine interior assent of the mind, which has the character of opinion rather than knowledge or faith, since the doctrine is to be accepted as true though with the awareness that it could possibly be false.[27] This assent may legitimately be withheld in certain cases, although to do so merely on the basis of one's own private judgment would be rash and dangerous.[28] However, assent *must* be withheld when the teaching in question clearly conflicts with any irreformable doctrine of the Church, i.e., a doctrine that has been taught infallibly. This is because, in the case of conflicting obligations, precedence must always be given to the stricter obligation (as the obligation to obey traffic laws may give way to the obligation to save lives); and the obligation to give definitive assent to the irreformable teaching of the infallible Church is a stricter obligation than the religious submission due to the non-infallible teaching of the authentic magisterium of the pope or bishops. This may be understood by analogy with the obligation of children to obey their parents. Just as children have a duty to obey their parents in all things, as long as their commands do not conflict with the higher law of God, so too the faithful children of the Church have a duty to accept the magisterial teaching of the pope and the bishops in union with him as long as their teaching does not conflict with the higher law of God's own revelation infallibly proposed by the Church.

The faithful must take care, therefore, to be well formed in the tradition of the Church, especially the sacred Scriptures, the

---

[27] See Thomas Aquinas, *De Veritate*, q. 14, a. 1.

[28] See: *Donum Veritatis*, §§24–31; Salaverri, *De Ecclesia Christi*, no. 675.

common teaching of the fathers and doctors, the divine liturgy, and the infallible decrees of prior popes and councils, so that they may not be led astray if the bishops, or the pope, or even an angel from heaven should preach a gospel contrary to that which has been received from the apostles (see Gal 1:8).

REPLY TO OBJECTION 1. To the first it must be said that when the pope or bishops exercise their merely authentic (non-infallible) magisterium, this is said to be the teaching "of the Church" only in an improper sense. When the pope teaches infallibly, then it can be said simply and properly that "the Church" teaches. But when the pope exercises his authentic magisterium without speaking infallibly, it should be said more properly that the pope teaches. And thus if he should err in such teaching, we would say that the pope has erred and not that the Church has erred. An indication of this can be seen in the concluding formula of the Profession of Faith, which speaks in the first two paragraphs of the definitive assent owed to the infallible teaching "of the Church," whereas the third paragraph speaks of the religious submission of will and intellect due to the non-definitive teaching "of the pope or college of bishops."[29]

REPLY TO OBJECTION 2. To the second it must be said that in the same series of general audiences devoted to a catechesis on the Church, Pope John Paul II distinguishes the ordinary (merely authentic) papal magisterium, which is exercised continually, from the extraordinary or solemn papal magisterium, which is exercised only in *ex cathedra* definitions,[30] and then proceeds to say that

---

[29] CDF, *Profession of Faith* (1998).

[30] Pope John Paul II, General Audience of March 10, 1993, §3 (English in "The Roman Pontiff is the Supreme Teacher," totus2us. com/teaching/jpii-catechesis-on-the-church/the-roman-pontiff -is-the-supreme-teacher/).

the pope is infallible "only when he speaks *ex cathedra.*"[31] But if the pope is infallible only when he speaks *ex cathedra*, then he is not infallible when he does not speak *ex cathedra*, and therefore he is able to teach error, even in matters of faith or morals, in his authentic magisterium when not speaking *ex cathedra.* In order to uphold the objection, one would have to deny what Pope John Paul II teaches here, which would be to attribute error to the teaching of his authentic magisterium in a matter pertaining to faith, in which case the objection would fail. Therefore, the charism of the Holy Spirit's assistance, about which the pope speaks in the passage quoted, cannot be understood as an absolute protection against error, such as is given in the case of infallible teaching, but should rather be understood as a grace of office, of which the pope must avail himself in order to benefit from it, just as grace is given to the justified so that they *would* not sin, but not so that they *could* not sin.

REPLY TO OBJECTION 3. To the third it must be said that this same religious submission is also due to the teaching of the individual bishops, who are certainly not infallible, as the Second Vatican Council teaches in *Lumen Gentium* §25 and as history also proves by the example of Nestorius and other heretical bishops. But if the response due to the teaching of individual bishops, who are not infallible, is this same religious assent or religious submission, then we cannot conclude that the authentic magisterium of the pope is infallible simply from the fact that a religious submission of will and intellect is owed to it.

REPLY TO OBJECTION 4. To the fourth it must be said that although the pope is the final judge in matters of faith and morals, he is not always acting *as* final judge even in his official teaching,

---

[31] Pope John Paul II, General Audience of March 24, 1993, §1.

but only when he speaks *ex cathedra.* Hence, if there should be controversy over a doctrine taught by the pope in the exercise of his merely authentic magisterium, whereby he proposes a doctrine of faith or morals as true, but not in the form of a solemn or final judgment, then the faithful are not left without recourse. They can appeal to the same pope (or a future pope) to issue a definitive judgment on the disputed point and so remove all doubts. And as long as the pope does not do so, it is clear that he does not demand an absolute assent to his teaching.

REPLY TO OBJECTION 5. To the fifth it must be said that this argument assumes that the First Vatican Council, by raising Cardinal Bellarmine's so-called "fourth opinion" to the status of a dogma, must also have dogmatized all the further reasons adduced by Bellarmine in support of his conclusion, of which one indeed was that extreme opinion of Albert Pighius which he calls "pious and probable." But this does not follow. And it is especially absurd to suppose that it entails an endorsement of precisely that opinion which Gasser explicitly *rejects* as being contained in the meaning of the definition when he says:

> As far as the doctrine set forth in the Draft goes, the deputation is unjustly accused of wanting to raise an extreme opinion, viz., that of Albert Pighius, to the dignity of a dogma. For the opinion of Albert Pighius, which Bellarmine indeed calls pious and probable, was that the Pope, as an individual person or a private teacher, was able to err from a type of ignorance but was never able to fall into heresy or teach heresy.... From this it appears that the doctrine in the proposed chapter is not that of Albert Pighius or the extreme opinion of any school, but rather that it is one and the same which Bellarmine teaches in the

place cited by the reverend speaker and which Bellarmine adduces in the fourth place and calls most certain and assured, or rather, correcting himself, the most common and certain opinion.[32]

Reply to Objection 6. To the sixth it must be said that this doctrinal commentary carries no properly juridical authority. For it was issued without the seal of papal approval by which, according to *Donum Veritatis* §18, the doctrinal decrees of the CDF participate in the ordinary (i.e., authentic) magisterium of the pope. It is therefore permissible for a Catholic theologian to hold that it simply errs on this point. Instead of describing propositions contrary to non-definitive magisterial teaching as *false*, it would be more accurate to describe all such propositions—and not only those of the prudential order—as *rash* or *dangerous* and therefore *not able to be safely taught*. For this would correspond more closely to the limited but real authority of the kind of teaching in question. That is, since it is not infallible, it could occasionally be false, and thus the contrary could be true; but because it is authoritative, there is a strong presumption of truth in its favor, on account of which it would be rash and dangerous to hold the contrary without sufficiently grave cause.

Reply to Objection 7. To the seventh it must be said that Cardinal Franzelin was concerned to emphasize the authority of the authentic papal magisterium against those who would consider themselves free to disregard everything except infallible teaching. But he failed to consider the possibility of authoritative papal teaching that would be in conflict with the previous teaching of the Church.

---

[32] Gasser, *Gift of Infallibility*, 58–59.

REPLY TO OBJECTION 8. To the eighth it must be said that this objection proves only that non-definitive doctrinal judgments *can* be true even in cases where they are later reversed due to changing circumstances. But it does not prove that they *must* be true, which would be required in order to uphold the thesis that the pope cannot err in the exercise of his authentic magisterium.

ARTICLE 3
Whether the Infallibility of the Pope Is Limited to the Exercise of His Extraordinary Magisterium?

OBJECTION 1. It seems that the infallibility of the pope is not limited to the exercise of his extraordinary magisterium, but extends also to his ordinary magisterium. For according to the Second Vatican Council, the pope as head of the Church possesses the same infallibility as the whole Church.[33] And the Church is infallible both in her solemn (or extraordinary) judgments and in her ordinary and universal magisterium.[34] Therefore, as Salaverri and many others have concluded, the pope must also be infallible both in his extraordinary judgments and in his ordinary magisterium.[35]

---

[33] See Vatican II, *Lumen Gentium*, §25; cf. Vatican I, *Pastor Aeternus*, ch. 4.

[34] See Vatican I, Dogmatic Constitution on the Catholic Faith, *Dei Filius* (1870), ch. 3; cf. Vatican II, *Lumen Gentium*, §25.

[35] See, for example, Salaverri, *Tractatus de Ecclesia Christi*, no. 647; Fenton, "Infallibility,"; J.M.A. Vacant, *Le magistère ordinaire de l'Eglise et ses organes* (Paris: Delhomme et Briguet, 1887); Edmond Dublanchy, "Infaillibilité du Pape," in *Dictionnaire de théologie catholique* (Paris: Letouzey et Ané, 1927), 7:1638–717; Paul Nau, "Le Magistère pontifical ordinaire au premier concile du Vatican," *Revue Thomiste* 62 (1962): 341–97. This was an argument I once defended: see John P. Joy, "*Cathedra Veritatis*: On the Extension

OBJECTION 2. Furthermore, as Salaverri points out,[36] the pope possesses the complete fullness of the supreme power of jurisdiction over the Church, which includes the power of the magisterium.[37] But if the pope were not infallible in his exercise of the ordinary magisterium, then he would not possess the complete fullness of magisterial power, since the gift of infallibility would then be more restricted in the pope than in the Church, for the Church is infallible in her ordinary and universal magisterium.

OBJECTION 3. Furthermore, according to Fenton,[38] the extraordinary magisterium is exercised only in "solemn" judgments.[39] But the pope is infallible whenever he speaks *ex cathedra*, and solemnity is not one of the conditions required for speaking *ex cathedra*.[40] Hence, the infallibility of the pope is not limited to extraordinary definitions—that is, those issued with special solemnity—but extends also to ordinary (i.e., non-solemn) *ex cathedra* definitions.

ON THE CONTRARY, according to Gasser's *relatio* on papal infallibility: "The pope is only infallible when, by a solemn judgment, he defines a matter of faith and morals for the Church universal."[41] But a solemn judgment is an exercise of the extraordinary magisterium; hence, the pope is infallible only in his extraordinary magisterium.

I ANSWER THAT, it must be said that the infallibility of the pope is limited to the exercise of his extraordinary magisterium.

---

of Papal Infallibility" (STL thesis, International Theological Institute, 2012), 51–89.

[36] Salaverri, *Tractatus de Ecclesia Christi*, no. 647.

[37] See Vatican I, *Pastor Aeternus*, ch. 4.

[38] See Fenton, "Infallibility," 188–89.

[39] See Vatican I, *Dei Filius*, ch. 3.

[40] See Vatican I, *Pastor Aeternus*, ch. 4.

[41] Gasser, *Gift of Infallibility*, 46.

The ordinary and universal magisterium, which is the magisterium of the whole Church dispersed throughout the world, is infallible when it proposes a doctrine of faith or morals "as to be believed as divinely revealed" or "as definitively to be held."[42] Now it is impossible that the pope should not likewise be infallible when he proposes doctrine in the same way, lest we fall into the error of the Gallicans by attributing greater authority to the Church than to the pope. But when the pope, as head of the universal Church, proposes a doctrine of faith or morals "as to be believed as divinely revealed" or "as definitively to be held," then he speaks *ex cathedra*, and this is reckoned as an exercise of the extraordinary magisterium. According to Pope Pius IX, the distinction between the ordinary and the extraordinary magisterium of the Church is this, that the extraordinary magisterium is exercised in "explicit decrees of ecumenical councils or Roman pontiffs," while the ordinary magisterium is exercised in the general teaching of "the whole Church dispersed throughout the world,"[43] on account of which the First Vatican Council described the ordinary magisterium as "universal."[44] The two modes of infallible teaching possessed by the bishops, therefore, pertain to the distinction between being gathered in council and being dispersed throughout the world; but no such distinction is possible for the singular person of the pope, and so he possesses only one mode of infallible teaching.

REPLY TO OBJECTION 1. To the first it must be said that this argument equivocates on the term "ordinary magisterium," which

---

[42] See: Vatican I, *Dei Filius*, ch. 3; Vatican II, *Lumen Gentium*, §25.

[43] Pope Pius IX, Apostolic Letter *Tuas Libenter* (1863).

[44] See Mansi, 51:322 B; cf. Salaverri, *Tractatus de Ecclesia Christi*, no. 552.

means one thing when applied to the Church and another thing when applied to the pope. Now the term "extraordinary magisterium" refers unequivocally to the explicit and definitive teaching of the Church—that is, the infallible teaching of the Church that is tangibly enshrined in public documents of the supreme magisterium. But because the extraordinary magisterium has two essential characteristics (namely, that it is both *explicit* and *definitive*), two very different forms of teaching can be contrasted against it and each will appear to be "ordinary" by comparison, though in different ways. First, and more properly, the term "ordinary magisterium" refers to the *definitive* but *non-explicit* teaching of the Church—that is, to the infallible teaching of the Church that is *not* found in explicit decrees of popes or councils but is gathered instead from all the sources of theology, and especially from the plain sense of Scripture, the consensus of the Church Fathers, the consensus of Catholic theologians, the consensus of the bishops, or the consensus of the faithful.[45] Secondly, however, the term "ordinary magisterium" is also sometimes used to refer to the *explicit* but *non-definitive* teaching of the pope or the college of bishops,[46] which is more properly called the "authentic magisterium" of the pope or bishops.[47] But since "ordinary" in this case simply *means* "non-definitive" or "non-infallible," it is

---

[45] See Joseph Kleutgen, *Die Theologie der Vorzeit verteidigt*, 2nd ed., vol. 1 (Münster: Theissing, 1867), 97–115. I explore this topic more thoroughly in John P. Joy, *On the Ordinary and Extraordinary Magisterium from Joseph Kleutgen to the Second Vatican Council*, Studia Oecumenica Friburgensia 84 (Münster: Aschendorff, 2017).

[46] See, for example: Pope Pius XII, Encyclical Letter *Humani Generis* (1950), §20; CDF, *Doctrinal Commentary*, §10.

[47] See Vatican II, *Lumen Gentium*, §25.

impossible for the pope to speak infallibly through his "ordinary" magisterium. This unfortunate ambiguity of the term "ordinary magisterium" has been a source of untold confusion.[48] It is as if one were to call an angel and an ape by the same name simply because neither is a man.

REPLY TO OBJECTION 2. To the second it must be said that the reason why the pope is not infallible in his ordinary magisterium is not because of a defect of magisterial power, but precisely on account of its fullness. The infallibility of the ordinary and universal magisterium of the Church arises from the consensus of individually fallible teachers proposing a doctrine of faith or morals as definitively to be held. But when the pope proposes a doctrine of faith or morals as definitively to be held, his teaching is infallible of itself and not by the consensus of the Church.

REPLY TO OBJECTION 3. To the third it must be said that, although it is true that solemnity is not a condition for infallible papal definitions, nevertheless the term "solemn" is not used *restrictively* in the expression "solemn judgment," as the objection supposes, but rather *descriptively*. That is, every infallible definition of doctrine, whether issued by pope or council, is intrinsically solemn, whether or not it is phrased in especially solemn language or issued with special solemnity of pomp and circumstance. There can be no *ex cathedra* definition which is not by that very fact a solemn judgment of the extraordinary magisterium.

---

[48] As Richard Gaillardetz rightly notes in this connection: "Contemporary discussions of issues related to the magisterium have been hampered considerably by a lack of terminological consistency" (Richard R. Gaillardetz, *Teaching with Authority: A Theology of the Magisterium of the Church,* Theology and Life, 41 [Collegeville, MN: Liturgical, 1997], 162n6).

ARTICLE 4
Whether the Pope Is Able to Speak Infallibly When He Confirms or Reaffirms a Doctrine Already Taught Infallibly by the Ordinary and Universal Magisterium?

OBJECTION 1. It seems that the pope is not able to speak infallibly when he confirms or reaffirms a doctrine already taught infallibly by the ordinary and universal magisterium. For according to the doctrinal commentary of the CDF on the concluding formula of the Profession of Faith: "*Such a doctrine can be confirmed or reaffirmed by the Roman Pontiff, even without recourse to a solemn definition....* The declaration of *confirmation or reaffirmation* by the Roman pontiff in this case is not a new dogmatic definition, but a formal attestation of a truth already possessed and infallibly transmitted by the Church."[49] Therefore, such acts of confirmation or reaffirmation of existing Catholic doctrine are not infallible.

OBJECTION 2. Furthermore, according to Cardinal Joseph Ratzinger, commenting on *Ordinatio Sacerdotalis*, "The Pope is not proposing any new dogmatic formula, but is confirming a certainty which has been constantly lived and held firm in the Church. In the technical language one should say: here we have an act of the ordinary magisterium of the Supreme Pontiff, an act therefore which is not a solemn definition *ex cathedra*."[50] But if *Ordinatio Sacerdotalis* belongs to the ordinary papal magisterium precisely because it does not propose any new dogmatic formula, then it must be the case that the pope is able to speak infallibly

---

[49] CDF, *Doctrinal Commentary*, §9 (italics original).

[50] Joseph Ratzinger, "The Limits of Church Authority," *L'Osservatore Romano* (English), June 29, 1994; cf. Ratzinger, "Letter Concerning the CDF Reply Regarding *Ordinatio Sacerdotalis*," *L'Osservatore Romano* (English), November 19, 1995.

only when defining new dogmas; and not, therefore, when confirming or reaffirming what has already been taught infallibly by the ordinary and universal magisterium.

OBJECTION 3. Furthermore, according to Archbishop Tarcisio Bertone, "If we were to hold that the Pope must necessarily make an *ex cathedra* definition whenever he intends to declare a doctrine as definitive because it belongs to the deposit of faith, it would imply an underestimation of the ordinary universal magisterium, and infallibility would be limited to the solemn definitions of the pope or a council."[51] Therefore, etc.

OBJECTION 4. Furthermore, the extraordinary magisterium of the pope is exercised in the act of solemn judgment, by which he settles controversies of faith. But if the pope confirms or reaffirms an existing Catholic doctrine, then he does not settle a controversy of faith, for there can be no controversy about a doctrine that has already been infallibly taught by the Church. Therefore, in such cases the pope does not exercise the extraordinary magisterium; and he is infallible only in his extraordinary magisterium, as shown above.

OBJECTION 5. Furthermore, it would be unnecessary to define infallibly a doctrine that has already been taught infallibly by the Church; and it would be unfitting for papal infallibility to be exercised unnecessarily; therefore, we ought not to suppose that the pope speaks infallibly when he confirms or reaffirms a doctrine already infallibly taught by the Church.

ON THE CONTRARY, there is the practice of the Church. For according to Pope Pius XII, the Assumption of Mary was already a dogma infallibly taught by the ordinary and universal

---

[51] Tarcisio Bertone, "Magisterial Documents and Public Dissent," *L'Osservatore Romano* (English), January 29, 1997.

magisterium before he proceeded to confirm it as such by a solemn definition.[52]

I ANSWER THAT it must be said that the pope is able to speak infallibly not only when he defines new dogmas, but also when he definitively confirms or reaffirms a doctrine already infallibly taught by the Church. For the purpose of the charism of infallibility bestowed on the pope by Christ is so that all Christ's faithful would be able to know with certainty what they ought to believe in order to be saved. But doubts may arise in the Church not only with regard to legitimately disputed questions, but also when the established teaching of the Church is obscured by heresies and errors. And indeed, the need for an infallible judgment is all the more urgent in the latter case. Thus the purpose of infallibility would be frustrated if the pope were not able to issue an infallible judgment by which he confirms or reaffirms existing Catholic doctrine.

Moreover, in order to avoid falling into the error of the Gallicans, we must hold that the charism of infallibility is not more restricted in the pope than in the Church, as said above. But it is clear from history that the Church is able to pronounce solemn and infallible definitions by which she confirms or reaffirms doctrines already taught infallibly by the ordinary and universal magisterium. For the Council of Nicaea solemnly defined the co-equal divinity of Christ, which had been infallibly taught by the ordinary and universal magisterium of the Church from the beginning, according to the words of Christ: "I and the Father are one" (John 10:30). Likewise, the Council of Trent defined the necessity of good works for salvation, which had always been

---

[52] See Pope Pius XII, Apostolic Constitution *Munificentissimus Deus* (1950), §12.

taught infallibly by the Church, according to the words of St. James: "You see then that a man is justified by works, and not by faith alone" (Jas 2:24). Therefore, the pope can also pronounce a solemn and infallible definition by which he confirms or reaffirms a doctrine already taught infallibly by the ordinary and universal magisterium, as Pope Pius XII did when he defined the dogma of the Assumption.

REPLY TO OBJECTION 1. To the first it must be said that this doctrinal commentary carries no properly juridical authority, as shown above. So it is permissible for a Catholic theologian to hold that the commentary simply errs on this point. Or perhaps one could also say that the commentary does not entirely exclude the possibility of a solemn definition confirming or reaffirming the infallible teaching of the Church, since it says only that this *can* be done without a solemn definition, thus leaving open the possibility that it could also be done with a solemn definition.

REPLY TO OBJECTION 2. To the second it must be said that there are no grounds for such a restriction of the extraordinary magisterium to the defining of *new* dogmas. This error seems to have arisen from a partial reading of Cardinal Billot, who describes an *ex cathedra* definition as a "new doctrinal judgment" and contrasts this with the way in which papal encyclical letters typically instruct the faithful about things already within the teaching of the Church.[53] However, Billot also proceeds to say that the term "defines," as it is used at Vatican I in the definition of papal infallibility, "is to be taken indiscriminately, whether about a thing never before defined, or about a thing already previously contained explicitly in the rule of the Church's magisterium, confirmed again by a new sentence and a new judgment

---

[53] See Billot, *Tractatus de Ecclesia Christi*, 640.

of the pope; just as we see practiced in the ecumenical councils with regard to the appearance of new errors or the return of old ones."[54] Hence, the solemn definition of a truth already infallibly taught by the Church is indeed a new judgment, but the only thing new about it is the *new act* of reaffirming the *same doctrine*.

REPLY TO OBJECTION 3. To the third it must be said that this argument would hold only if the same doctrine could not be infallibly taught more than once, but there is no reason to suppose such a limitation. And in fact, many doctrines have been taught infallibly more than once. For example, that the Sacred Scriptures are divinely inspired has always been taught infallibly by the ordinary and universal magisterium, according to the words of Saint Paul: "All Scripture is inspired by God" (2 Tim 3:16); and yet this was solemnly defined both at Florence and at Trent, according to the words of Pope Leo XIII: "This is the ancient and unchanging faith of the Church, solemnly defined in the Councils of Florence and of Trent."[55]

REPLY TO OBJECTION 4. To the fourth it must be said that the solemn judgments of popes and ecumenical councils are always *sufficient* to settle controversies of faith, but it is not *necessary* that there be an actual controversy of faith, much less a legitimate one, in order for a solemn judgment to be given. According to Gasser's *relatio*, the forty-seventh proposed emendation to the text of the definition of papal infallibility had to be rejected for this reason: "The reverend Father appears to restrict pontifical infallibility only to controversies of faith, whereas the Pontiff is also

---

[54] Billot, *Tractatus de Ecclesia Christi*, 640–41.
[55] Pope Leo XIII, Encyclical Letter *Providentissimus Deus* (1893), §20.

infallible as universal teacher and as supreme witness of tradition, the deposit of faith."[56]

REPLY TO OBJECTION 5. To the fifth it must be said that this objection neglects the essentially pastoral purpose of the magisterium. As Joseph Kleutgen says:

> Something can be universally taught and believed in the Church as revealed truth, and therefore the error opposing it can be rejected with certainty as heretical, and yet a judgment of the Church can still be necessary if the innovators succeed in winning a following, or in seducing even a single prominent member of the Church, or other men of great prestige, such that it is slightly doubtful, especially for the multitude of the faithful, upon which side the truth lies.[57]

Solemn judgments that confirm or reaffirm existing Catholic doctrine may not be necessary for the advance of sacred theology; but they are often very necessary for the salvation of souls, and that is the primary purpose of the magisterium.

ARTICLE 5
Whether the Infallibility of the Pope Is Limited to Defining Dogmas of Divine and Catholic Faith?

OBJECTION 1. It seems that the infallibility of the pope is limited to defining dogmas of divine and Catholic faith—that is, to the primary object of the magisterium. For according to Bishop Joseph Fessler, in his book on the infallibility of the pope, for which he received a personal letter of thanks from Pope Pius IX, the pope is infallible only when he defines truths *as divinely revealed* or

---

[56] Gasser, *Gift of Infallibility*, 74.
[57] Kleutgen, *Die Theologie*, 100.

when he condemns errors *as heretical*,[58] both of which pertain exclusively to the primary object of the magisterium.

OBJECTION 2. Furthermore, according to Gasser's *relatio*, Vatican I left the question of the secondary object of infallibility in the same state in which it was before,[59] and this was a state of free theological opinion.[60] Hence, it cannot be conclusively asserted that papal infallibility extends beyond the definition of dogma or the condemnation of heresy.

OBJECTION 3. Furthermore, the teaching of the Second Vatican Council is commonly held to be non-infallible precisely because it did not define any new dogmas or condemn any errors specifically as heretical.[61] And the infallibility of the pope is the same as that of the Church, as said above.

ON THE CONTRARY, according to the CDF it is a matter of Catholic doctrine that "the infallibility of the Church's magisterium extends not only to the deposit of faith," which is the primary object of the magisterium, "but also to those matters without

---

[58] See Joseph Fessler, *Die wahre und die falsche Unfehlbarkeit der Päpste* (Vienna: Sartori, 1871).

[59] See Gasser, *Gift of Infallibility*, 80.

[60] See Cuthbert Butler, *The Vatican Council*, vol. 2 (London: Longmans and Green, 1930), 216.

[61] See, for example: Umberto Betti, "Qualification théologique de la Constitution," in *L'Église de Vatican II*, vol. 2, ed. Guilherme Baraúna (Paris: Cerf, 1967), 217; Yves Congar, "En guise de conclusion," in *L'Église de Vatican II*, vol. 3 (Paris: Cerf, 1967), 1367; Francis A. Sullivan, *Magisterium: Teaching Authority in the Catholic Church* (Eugene: Wipf & Stock, 2002), 121; Sullivan, *Creative Fidelity: Weighing and Interpreting the Documents of the Magisterium* (Eugene: Wipf & Stock, 2003), 167; Avery Dulles, *Magisterium: Teacher and Guardian of the Faith* (Naples, FL: Sapientia Press, 2007), 69–70, 76.

which that deposit cannot be rightly preserved and expounded,"[62] which refers to the secondary object of the magisterium.

I ANSWER THAT, it must be said that the pope is able to speak infallibly not only in defining divinely revealed truths as dogmas of divine and Catholic faith, but also in defining matters of faith or morals that are necessarily connected to divine revelation. Here it should be noted that the primary object of the magisterium comprises every doctrine directly revealed by God and contained in the deposit of faith—namely, in Scripture or Tradition. Such doctrines can be infallibly defined by the pope as dogmas which must be believed by divine and Catholic faith (*de fide credenda*), the obstinate doubt or denial of which constitutes heresy.[63] Such dogmas can also be defined negatively by the definitive condemnation of the opposing heresy.

The secondary object of the magisterium comprises those truths pertaining to faith or morals that are not directly revealed, but are intrinsically connected to divine revelation by a logical or historical relationship and which are required for inviolately preserving and faithfully expounding the deposit of faith.[64] Truths contained in the secondary object of the magisterium include philosophical truths presupposed to divine revelation, such as the existence of God, the immortality of the human soul, and the mind's ability to know truth with certainty; theological conclusions that follow logically from divine revelation by the aid of natural reason; and dogmatic facts, such as the legitimacy of an ecumenical council or the validity of a papal election. Such

---

[62] CDF, Declaration in Defense of the Catholic Doctrine on the Church *Mysterium Ecclesiae* (1973), §3.

[63] John Paul II, *Codex Iuris Canonici* [henceforth: 1983 *CIC*] (Vatican City: Typis Polyglottis Vaticanis, 1983), can. 751.

[64] See John Paul II, Motu Proprio *Ad Tuendam Fidem* (1998), §§3–4.

truths can be infallibly defined by the pope as doctrines which must be held definitively (*de fide tenenda*). Although the denial of such doctrines would not constitute heresy in the strict sense, the doctrinal commentary of the CDF on the Profession of Faith says: "Whoever denies these truths would be in a position of rejecting a truth of Catholic doctrine and would therefore no longer be in full communion with the Catholic Church."[65] Such truths of Catholic doctrine can also be defined negatively by the definitive condemnation of the opposing error as false or proximate to heresy.

The extension of infallibility to the secondary object of the magisterium is taught by the Second Vatican Council, which says: "And this infallibility with which the divine Redeemer willed his Church to be endowed in defining doctrine of faith and morals, extends as far as the deposit of revelation extends, which must be guarded inviolately and expounded faithfully."[66] For according to the Theological Commission's official explanation of this text, "The object of the infallibility of the Church, thus explained, has the same extension as the revealed deposit; and therefore it extends to all those things, and only to those things, which either directly pertain to the revealed deposit itself, or which are required for the same deposit to be inviolably guarded and faithfully expounded."[67] And if the infallibility of the Church extends to the secondary object of the magisterium, then so does the infallibility of the pope. For the pope possesses the very same infallibility as that possessed by the Church, as shown above.

REPLY TO OBJECTION 1. To the first it must be said that a semi-official letter of approbation for Fessler's work as a whole

---

[65] CDF, *Doctrinal Commentary*, §6; cf. 1983 *CIC*, can. 750, §2.

[66] Vatican II, *Lumen Gentium*, §25.

[67] *Acta Synodalia* 3/1:251.

does not necessarily imply an endorsement of every claim made within the work. And Gasser's *relatio* explicitly denies that papal infallibility is limited to the definition of dogma and the condemnation of heresy in the way that Fessler would have it. For according to Gasser:

> The Deputation *de fide* is not of the mind that this word ["defines"] should be understood in a juridical sense [*in sensu forensi*] so that it only signifies putting an end to controversy which has arisen in respect to heresy and doctrine which is properly speaking *de fide*. Rather, the word "defines" signifies that the pope directly and conclusively pronounces his sentence about a doctrine that concerns matters of faith or morals and does so in such a way that each one of the faithful can be certain of the mind of the Apostolic See, of the mind of the Roman pontiff; in such a way, indeed, that he or she knows for certain that such and such a doctrine is held to be heretical, proximate to heresy, certain or erroneous, et cetera, by the Roman pontiff. Such, therefore, is the meaning of the word "defines."[68]

REPLY TO OBJECTION 2. To the second it must be said that the question left unsettled by Vatican I was not whether the infallibility of the pope extends to the secondary object, but rather whether this secondary extension of infallibility is itself a dogma or "merely" theologically certain. This indeed remains an open question. But there can be no doubt that the extension of papal infallibility to the secondary object of the magisterium is at least a theologically certain conclusion and not merely a matter of free

[68] Gasser, *Gift of Infallibility*, 92.

theological opinion. Moreover, the constant consensus of Catholic theologians regarding the certitude of this doctrine is sufficient evidence that it is to be held definitively in virtue of the infallible teaching of the ordinary and universal magisterium.

REPLY TO OBJECTION 3. To the third it must be said that this common opinion about Vatican II is not well-founded. It appears to arise from three sources. First, there is the example of prominent authors such as Fessler who arbitrarily limit papal infallibility to the primary object of the magisterium, as shown above. Second, there is the wording of the 1917 *Code of Canon Law*, which said: "Nothing is to be understood as dogmatically declared or defined unless this is clearly manifested."[69] Now the word "dogmatically" can be used in a broad sense to mean something like "fixedly" or "irreformably," but it also has a narrower technical meaning which refers exclusively to the primary object of the magisterium. And so it seems to have been interpreted by many. But this is corrected in the 1983 *Code of Canon Law*, which substitutes "infallibly" for "dogmatically" so that the parallel canon now reads: "Nothing is to be understood as infallibly defined unless this is manifestly the case."[70] Third, there are the words of Pope Paul VI, who said that the council "did not wish to issue extraordinary dogmatic pronouncements,"[71] and again, that it "avoided giving solemn dogmatic definitions backed by the infallibility of the Church's magisterium," and "avoided pronouncing in an extraordinary way dogmas endowed with the note

---

[69] Benedict XV, *Codex Iuris Canonici* [hereafter: 1917 *CIC*] (Vatican City: Typis Polyglottis Vaticanis, 1917), can. 1323, §3.

[70] 1983 *CIC*, can. 749, §3.

[71] Pope Paul VI, Address During the Last General Meeting of the Second Vatican Council, December 7, 1965.

of infallibility."[72] But if Paul VI is using the terms "dogma" and "dogmatic" in the broader sense of "definitive," then we cannot infer from his words any restriction of infallibility to the primary object of the magisterium. And if he is using them in the stricter sense, then we can infer from them only that Vatican II did not in fact infallibly define any dogmas (*de fide credenda*), but not that it did not define (much less could not have defined) any truths of Catholic doctrine (*de fide tenenda*).

ARTICLE 6

Whether the Infallibility of the Pope Extends to the Canonization of Saints?[73]

OBJECTION 1. It seems that the infallibility of the pope does not extend to the canonization of saints. For according to John Lamont, in order to teach infallibly, the pope "must assert that his teaching is a final decision that binds the whole Church to believe in its contents upon pain of sin against faith."[74] But in the formula of canonization, as Lamont says:

> There is no mention of teaching a question of faith or morals, no requirement that the faithful believe or confess the statement being proclaimed, and no assertion that a

---

[72] Pope Paul VI, General Audience of January 12, 1966 (translation mine).

[73] For arguments against the conclusion reached in this article, see the collection of essays edited by Peter Kwasniewski, *Are Canonizations Infallible? Revisiting a Disputed Question* (Waterloo, ON: Arouca Press, 2021).

[74] John R. T. Lamont, "The Authority of Canonizations," *Rorate Caeli*, Aug. 24, 2018, rorate-caeli.blogspot.com/2018/08/the-authority-of-canonizations-do-all.html; also published in the aforementioned *Are Canonizations Infallible?*, 151–62.

denial of the proclamation is heretical, subject to anathema, or entails separation from the unity of the Church. The absence of these condemnations is itself an absence of the condition of the intent to bind the whole Church in the sense required for an infallible teaching, because these assertions are what constitute binding the Church in this sense.[75]

OBJECTION 2. Furthermore, the infallibility of the Church extends only to matters of faith or morals that are either contained in divine revelation or so closely connected with the deposit of faith that "revelation would be imperiled unless an absolutely certain decision could be made about them."[76] Now the sanctity of any particular post-apostolic Christian cannot possibly be contained in divine revelation; nor is it necessarily connected with divine revelation unless "the doctrine of a particular saint has been so extensively adopted by the infallible teaching of the Church that denial of his sanctity would cast doubt upon the teachings themselves" or unless "devotion to a saint has been so widespread and important in the Church that the denial of that individual's sanctity would cast doubt upon the role of the Holy Spirit in guiding the Church."[77] But these conditions are not realized in many canonizations. Therefore, canonizations are not necessarily infallible.

OBJECTION 3. Furthermore, recent changes in the process of examining causes for canonization, such as the abolition of the so-called devil's advocate and the reduction in the number of miracles required, have considerably lessened the reliability

[75] Ibid., 155.
[76] Ibid., 157, citing Van Noort.
[77] Ibid., 159.

of these examinations, so that even if canonizations used to be infallible, they cannot be so any longer.

OBJECTION 4. Furthermore, in the ceremony of canonization there are prayers for the truthfulness of the decree of canonization, which implies the possibility that the decree could be false.

ON THE CONTRARY, according to Saint Thomas Aquinas: "The honor we show the saints is a certain profession of faith by which we believe in their glory, and it is to be piously believed that even in this the judgment of the Church is not able to err."[78]

I ANSWER THAT, it must be said that we ought to hold that the infallibility of the pope extends to the canonization of saints. In the first place, it is clear that the pope is issuing a solemn judgment as supreme head of the universal Church when he pronounces a typical formula of canonization, which is as follows: "For the honor of the blessed Trinity, the exaltation of the Catholic faith, and the increase of the Christian life, by the authority of our Lord Jesus Christ, and of the holy apostles Peter and Paul, and our own, we declare and define that N. is a saint and we enroll him among the saints, decreeing that he is to be venerated as such by the whole Church."

Hence, the only question that arises is whether the canonization of saints falls within the object of the infallible magisterium as a matter of faith or morals. And here it must be said that the canonization of the saints is intrinsically connected with the holiness of the Church, which is one of the essential marks of the Church, and so falls within the secondary object of infallibility. For by the act of canonizing a saint, the pope not only declares that this saint is in heaven, but also establishes the liturgical veneration of this saint, so that the most holy sacrifice of the Mass

---

[78] Thomas Aquinas, *Quodlibet* IX, q. 8, a. 16.

should henceforth be offered in honor of this saint. And it would be contrary to the holiness of the Church if the whole Church would be obliged to venerate and to offer Masses in honor of a soul not in heaven.

Moreover, according to Salaverri, the infallibility of the pope in canonizing saints has been implicitly defined.[79] For on several occasions, the supreme pontiffs have expressly declared the infallibility of these judgments. For example, Pope Pius XI says: "We, as the supreme teacher of the Catholic Church, pronounce infallible judgment with these words." And again: "We, from the chair of blessed Peter, as the supreme teacher of the whole Church of Christ, solemnly proclaim with these words an infallible judgment." Likewise, Pope Pius XII: "We, the universal teacher of the Catholic Church, from the one chair founded on Peter by the word of the Lord, have solemnly pronounced with these words this judgment, knowing that it cannot be wrong."[80] Therefore, although it would not be heretical in the strict sense to deny the infallibility of the canonization of saints, it would be contrary not only to the common teaching of Catholic theologians but also to the express teaching of Popes Pius XI and Pius XII.

REPLY TO OBJECTION 1. To the first it must be said that the definitive and binding character of the decree of canonization is sufficiently manifest in the formula of canonization through the use of the word *definimus* ("we define"). Lamont, however, objects that the presence of the word *definimus* in the formula of canonization is not decisive, saying:

---

[79] See Salaverri, *Tractatus de Ecclesia Christi*, no. 726.

[80] All cited in Salaverri, *Tractatus de Ecclesia Christi*, no. 725 (trans. Kenneth Baker in *Sacrae Theologiae Summa*, vol. 1B [Saddle River, NJ: Keep the Faith, 2015], 273.

Nor can we suppose that the use of the Latin word *definimus* necessarily signifies the act of defining a doctrine of the faith. The word has a more general, juridical sense of ruling on some controversy concerning faith or morals. This general sense was recognized by the fathers of the First Vatican Council, and explicitly distinguished by them from the specific sense of *definio* that obtains in infallible definitions.[81]

But this is the reverse of the truth. As we have already seen, the official *relatio* on infallibility does indeed distinguish between a broader and a narrower sense of the word "defines"; but it is the narrower sense which Gasser describes as "juridical" and which he rejects, while affirming that the broader meaning of the word obtains in infallible definitions, as noted above (a. 5, reply to obj. 1).

REPLY TO OBJECTION 2. To the second it must be said that the canonization of every saint is sufficiently connected to divine revelation in precisely the way that the objection maintains on behalf of only some saints. That is, just as the denial of the sanctity of a saint who has already been widely venerated in the Church would cast doubt upon the role of the Holy Spirit in guiding the Church, so also would the denial of the sanctity of one whose veneration has been decreed for the whole Church for the future.

REPLY TO OBJECTION 3. To the third it must be said that the charism of infallibility rests on the promise of God, not on the reliability of the process. As such it guarantees only the truth of the final definition, not the prudence of making it. Just as the pope, when he intends to define a dogma of faith, ought carefully to investigate the sources of revelation in order to be certain of the truth he intends to define, so also, when he intends to canonize a

---

[81] Lamont, "Authority of Canonizations," 156.

saint, he ought carefully to investigate the sanctity of that person in life and the miracles worked by him after his death. Failure to do so places himself at risk of being directly prevented by divine intervention, but it does not cast doubt on the certainty of the canonization itself, if God in his providence has allowed him to pronounce it. For then the words of Christ apply: "Whatever you bind on earth shall be bound in heaven, and whatever you loose on earth shall be loosed in heaven" (Mt 16:19).

REPLY TO OBJECTION 4. To the fourth it must be said that prayers for the truthfulness of the decree are inconclusive since there is nothing unfitting in asking God to do that which he has promised to do.

ARTICLE 7
Whether the Pope Is Able to Speak Infallibly without Explicitly Addressing the Universal Church?

OBJECTION 1. It seems that the pope is not able to speak infallibly when he does not explicitly address his teaching to the universal Church. For as Gasser's *relatio* makes clear, the pope is said to be infallible only when he teaches as supreme head of the Church and "not, first of all, when he decrees something as a private teacher, nor only as the bishop and ordinary of a particular See and province."[82] But if the pope addresses his teaching only to a part of the Church, then he may be acting only as local bishop of Rome, or Primate of Italy, or Patriarch of the West, and not as head of the universal Church.

OBJECTION 2. Furthermore, according to the definition itself, the pope is said to be infallible only when he defines a doctrine

---

[82] Gasser, *Gift of Infallibility*, 77.

as one that is "to be held by the whole Church,"[83] which he cannot do if he does not address his teaching to the whole Church.

ON THE CONTRARY, according to Cardinal Billot: "It is not necessary for a papal document to be materially directed to all the bishops or faithful; it is enough that it pertains to the deposit of faith and there is present the manifest intention of putting an end to doubt by a definitive sentence not subject to further determination."[84]

I ANSWER THAT, it must be said that, in order to speak infallibly, the pope must be acting as supreme head of the whole Church. This is most clearly manifest when the pope explicitly addresses the whole Church, as he frequently does in his apostolic constitutions and encyclical letters. But this can be made manifest in other ways. For example, in the encyclical letter *Commissum Divinitus*, which is addressed only to the clergy of Switzerland, Pope Gregory XVI explicitly invokes his supreme apostolic authority, which he does not possess otherwise than as head of the whole Church, when he infallibly condemns the Baden articles as follows:

> With the fullness of the apostolic power, We reprove and condemn the aforementioned articles of the meeting of Baden as containing false, rash, and erroneous assertions; as detracting from the rights of the Holy See, overthrowing the government of the Church and its divine constitution, and subjecting the ecclesiastical ministry to secular domination; and as proceeding from condemned premises. We decree that they should forever be considered condemned.[85]

---

[83] Vatican I, *Pastor Aeternus*, ch. 4.

[84] Billot, *Tractatus de Ecclesia Christi*, 642.

[85] Pope Gregory XVI, Encyclical Letter *Commissum Divinitus* (1835), §16.

Similarly, when the pope imposes a profession of faith on any individual or group as a condition for union with the Church, it is clear that he is acting as supreme head of the universal Church, as, for example, in the professions of faith prescribed by Pope Hormisdas for the Acacians (517), by Pope Innocent III for the Waldensians (1208), by Pope Gregory XIII for the Greeks (1575), or by Pope Benedict XIV for the Maronites (1743). For it is only as supreme head of the Church that he has the authority to determine the conditions for union with the Church.

OBJECTION 1. To the first it must be said that it is true that the pope *may* be acting only as the local bishop of Rome, or Primate of Italy, or Patriarch of the West in such cases. But he need not always be acting only in these more limited capacities, as is clear from what is said above.

OBJECTION 2. To the second it must be said that if the pope, acting in his capacity as supreme teacher of the universal Church, imposes a doctrine of faith or morals on any part of the Church directly, then by that very fact he also indirectly imposes the same doctrine on the whole Church.

On Particular Cases of Papal Teaching

THE PREVIOUS QUESTION considered the extension and limits of papal infallibility in general by means of a close examination of the criteria set forth at Vatican I respecting the subject, the object, and the act of infallible papal teaching. It remains in this question to consider whether the necessary criteria are fulfilled in particular cases of papal teaching. Although all Catholics agree in principle that the pope can teach infallibly in certain circumstances (as defined at Vatican I), there is much less agreement about how often and in what particular cases he has done so in practice. At one extreme, there are those who hold that the popes have spoken infallibly only twice, in defining the dogmas of the Immaculate Conception (1854) and Assumption (1950) of the Blessed Virgin Mary. At the other extreme, there are those who hold that everything the pope teaches in an official capacity in matters of faith or morals is at least practically infallible.

Regarding particular cases of papal teaching, there are twelve questions to be considered: (1) whether there have been more than two infallible papal definitions in the history of the Church; (2) whether the pope speaks infallibly in *Dominus Iesus*; (3) whether the pope speaks infallibly in *Evangelium Vitae*; (4) whether the pope speaks infallibly in *Ordinatio Sacerdotalis*; (5) whether the pope speaks infallibly in *Veritatis Splendor*; (6) whether the *Credo* of Paul VI is an infallible profession of faith; (7) whether the pope speaks infallibly in *Humanae Vitae*; (8) whether the "Oath against Modernism" is an infallible profession of faith; (9) whether the pope speaks infallibly in *Quanta Cura*; (10) whether the pope speaks infallibly in *Providentissimus Deus*; (11) whether the pope speaks infallibly in *Exsurge Domine*; (12) whether the pope speaks infallibly in *Unam Sanctam*.

ARTICLE I
Whether There Have Been More Than Two Infallible Papal Definitions?

OBJECTION 1. It seems that there have not been more than two infallible papal definitions in the history of the Church. For according to the common statement of the Lutheran-Roman Catholic Dialogue on teaching authority and infallibility in the Church: "There are only two papal pronouncements which are generally acknowledged by Catholics as having engaged papal infallibility: the dogma of the Immaculate Conception (1854) and that of the Assumption of the Blessed Virgin (1950)."[86] But if any other papal pronouncement had engaged papal infallibility, this fact would be generally acknowledged by Catholics.

OBJECTION 2. Furthermore, according to the *Code of Canon Law*: "No doctrine is understood to be defined infallibly unless this is manifestly evident."[87] But as the common statement of the Lutheran-Roman Catholic Dialogue notes, the infallible character of a papal pronouncement is not manifestly evident

---

[86] Lutheran-Roman Catholic Dialogue [henceforth: LRCD], "Teaching Authority and Infallibility in the Church: Common Statement," *Theological Studies* 40 (1979): 148.

[87] 1983 *CIC*, can. 749, §3.

unless it claims infallibility for itself.[88] And this does not occur outside the two definitions of Marian dogma mentioned above.

ON THE CONTRARY, according to the official *relatio* on papal infallibility: "Thousands and thousands of dogmatic judgments have already gone forth from the Apostolic See."[89]

I ANSWER THAT, it must be said that there have certainly been more than two infallible papal definitions in the history of the Church. The CDF gives six examples in its commentary on the concluding formula of the Profession of Faith: *Benedictus Deus* (1336) on the immortality of the spiritual soul and its immediate recompense after death; *Ineffabilis Deus* (1854) on the Immaculate Conception of Mary; *Providentissimus Deus* (1893) on the inspiration and inerrancy of Scripture; *Apostolicae Curae* (1896) on the invalidity of Anglican orders; *Munificentissimus Deus* (1950) on the Assumption of Mary; and *Evangelium Vitae* (1995) on the grave immorality of murder.[90]

The Jesuit theologian Klaus Schatz, even though arbitrarily limiting his search to properly dogmatic definitions, recognizes seven instances of infallible papal teaching: the tome of Pope Leo the Great to Flavian of Constantinople (449); the dogmatic epistle of Pope Agatho to Emperor Constantine IV (680); *Cum Occasione* (1653), condemning five propositions of Cornelius Jansen as heretical; *Auctorem Fidei* (1794), which condemns eighty-five errors of the Synod of Pistoia, seven specifically as heretical; as well as the aforementioned definitions of *Benedictus Deus* (1336), *Ineffabilis Deus* (1854); and *Munificentissimus Deus* (1950).[91]

---

[88] See LRCD, "Teaching Authority," 149.

[89] Mansi, 52:1215 A.

[90] See CDF, *Doctrinal Commentary*, §11.

[91] See Klaus Schatz, "Welche bisherigen päpstlichen Lehrentscheidungen sind '*ex cathedra*'? Historische und theologische

The eminent ecclesiologist Louis Billot gives eleven examples: in addition to several of the aforementioned, he includes *Unam Sanctam* (1302) on the necessity for salvation of being subject to the Roman Pontiff; *Exsurge Domine* (1520), condemning the errors of Martin Luther; *Caelestis Pastor* (1687), condemning the errors of Miguel de Molinos; *Cum Alias* (1699), condemning the errors of François de Fénelon; *Unigenitus Dei Filius* (1713), condemning the errors of Pasquier Quesnel; and *Quanta Cura* (1864), condemning current errors.[92]

Edmond Dublanchy gives a very similar list in the entry on papal infallibility in the monumental *Dictionnaire de Théologie Catholique*, although he hesitates over *Quanta Cura*. He also discusses, but ultimately leaves open, the possibility of including *Pascendi Dominici Gregis* (1907), on the doctrines of the modernists, and *Lamentabili Sane* (1907), condemning the errors of the modernists.[93]

Salaverri provides a list drawn up from the historical investigations of Carlos da Silva Tarouca of twenty *ex cathedra* definitions from the first millennium alone.[94]

Although none of these lists can claim to be definitive (nor exhaustive), to maintain that there have only been two instances of popes speaking infallibly can only be based on ignorance of history.

Überlegungen," in *Dogmengeschichte und katholische Theologie*, ed. Werner Löser, Karl Lehmann, and Matthias Lutz-Bachmann (Würzburg: Echter, 1985), 402–22; see also Sullivan, *Creative Fidelity*, 82–89.

[92] See Billot, *Tractatus de Ecclesia Christi*, 642–44.

[93] See Dublanchy, "Infaillibilité," 1703–4.

[94] See Carlos da Silva Tarouca, *Institutiones historiae ecclesiasticae: Ecclesia in imperio Romano-Byzantino* (Rome: Gregorian University, 1933), 86–190; see also Salaverri, *Tractatus de Ecclesia Christi*, nos. 623–29.

REPLY TO OBJECTION 1. To the first it should be said that this statement represents no more than a common opinion of modern Catholics, which is not the same as the genuine *consensus fidelium*. This common opinion has been widely fostered and eagerly received by many who are eager to minimize the doctrine of papal infallibility in the hopes of easing ecumenical relations with those who reject the primacy of the pope. Although well intentioned, such an approach is misguided since true unity must be firmly rooted in truth.

REPLY TO OBJECTION 2. To the second it should be said that even these two definitions of Marian dogma do not explicitly claim infallibility for themselves, and thus according to this criterion there would be no historical instances of popes speaking *ex cathedra*, which is absurd. What is required for the pope to speak *ex cathedra* is not that he claim or even intend to speak infallibly, but that he intend to speak definitively.

ARTICLE 2
Whether the Pope Speaks Infallibly in *Dominus Iesus*?

OBJECTION 1. It seems that the pope does not speak infallibly in the declaration *Dominus Iesus* (2000). For this declaration was issued by the CDF, and according to Salaverri, the CDF is not able to participate in the infallible exercise of the papal magisterium.[95]

OBJECTION 2. Furthermore, in order for *Dominus Iesus* to be infallible, the gift of infallibility would have to be communicated from the pope to the CDF. But the gift of infallibility is not able to be communicated, according to the words of Bishop

---

[95] See Salaverri, *Tractatus de Ecclesia Christi*, no. 665; see also Sullivan, *Creative Fidelity*, 19–20.

Gasser: "How can infallibility be communicated? This I do not understand."[96]

OBJECTION 3. Furthermore, according to Richard Gaillardetz: "While canon law envisions the participation of the Roman curia in papal governance of the Church, there is reason to question whether the curia can similarly participate in the doctrinal teaching authority of the pope. This authority cannot be delegated because it is his by virtue of his episcopal office as bishop of Rome."[97] Much less, therefore, can the infallible exercise of the papal magisterium be delegated to the CDF.

ON THE CONTRARY, according to Bishop Angelo Amato, this declaration "was explicitly approved by the Supreme Pontiff with a formula of special authority.... It re-proposes truths of divine Catholic faith and doctrinal truths to be firmly followed. Hence, the assent requested of the faithful is definitive and irrevocable."[98] But definitive and irrevocable assent are required only in response to infallible teaching.

I ANSWER THAT, it must be said that, in the declaration *Dominus Iesus*, the necessary conditions pertaining to the object and act of infallibility are clearly fulfilled, for various doctrines pertaining to faith are proposed explicitly as *to be firmly believed or held*. The only question, therefore, concerns the condition pertaining to the subject of papal infallibility, since this document was promulgated by the CDF and not directly by the pope himself; and although

---

[96] Mansi, 52:1216 C.

[97] Gaillardetz, *Teaching with Authority*, 287.

[98] Cited by Matthew W. I. Dunn, "The CDF's Declaration *Dominus Iesus* and Pope John Paul II," *Louvain Studies* 36 (2012): 66, with reference to Angelo Amato, "The *Dominus Iesus* and the Other Religions," *Pro Dialogo: Pontificium Consilium pro Dialogo inter Religiones* 126 (2007): 234.

the CDF is able to participate in the ordinary (authentic) mag-isterium of the pope,[99] it is generally held that the CDF is not able to participate in the infallible papal magisterium.

However, the documents of the CDF can be approved by the pope either in a common form (*in forma communi*) or in a specific form (*in forma specifica*). When such a document is approved in the common form, it remains a document of the CDF; but if it is approved in the specific form, it then becomes a properly pontifical act.[100] Hence, there is nothing to prevent the pope from defining doctrine infallibly in a document of the CDF that he approves in the specific form. And this accords with the words of Pope Pius IX, where he says that dogmas of divine faith can be "defined by the explicit decrees of ecumenical councils or of Roman pontiffs and of this Apostolic See."[101] For what would be the purpose of mentioning the decrees of the Apostolic See in addition to those of the Roman pontiffs, unless he speaks of the doctrinal decrees of the Roman Congregations?

Now the declaration *Dominus Iesus* was approved by the pope in the specific form, as Matthew Dunn shows.[102] Traditionally, approval in the specific form has been indicated by phrases such as *motu proprio*, or *plenitudine suae potestatis*, or especially *ex certa scientia*.[103] Now the formula of approval appended to *Dominus Iesus*

---

[99] See CDF, *Donum Veritatis*, §18.

[100] See Dulles, *Magisterium*, 53; see also John M. Huels, "Interpreting an Instruction Approved *In Forma Specifica*," *Studia Canonica* 32 (March 1998): 5–46.

[101] Pius IX, *Tuas Libenter*.

[102] See Dunn, "The CDF's Declaration *Dominus Iesus*," 46–75.

[103] Dunn, "The CDF's Declaration *Dominus Iesus*," 65; see also: *New Commentary on the Code of Canon Law*, ed. John P. Beal et al. (New York: Paulist Press, 2000), 58; Valentín Gómez-Iglesias,

is as follows: "The supreme pontiff John Paul II, in an audience granted to the undersigned Cardinal Prefect of the Congregation for the Doctrine of the Faith, on June 16, 2000, with certain knowledge (*certa scientia*) and by his apostolic authority (*et auctoritate sua apostolica*), ratified (*ratam*) and confirmed (*confirmavit*) this declaration, adopted in plenary session, and ordered its publication."[104] By contrast, a typical formula of approval in the common form is as follows: "The sovereign pontiff, at the audience granted to the undersigned Cardinal Prefect, approved the present document, adopted in ordinary session of this congregation, and ordered its publication."[105]

It may be objected that the formula of approval appended to *Dominus Iesus* does not use the precise phrase "*in forma specifica approbavit,*" which it ought to do, according to the General Regulations of the Roman Curia promulgated in 1992.[106] However, as advisable as it may be for the pope to observe such a rule in order that his intentions may be more clearly manifest, this rule cannot prevent the pope from using other traditional formulae to indicate his intention to approve a document in the specific form. That it was the pope's intention to approve this document in the specific form can also be confirmed by his words in an Angelus address given later in the same year, where he says: "With the Declaration *Dominus Iesus*—Jesus is Lord—approved by me in a special way (*approvata da me in forma speciale*) at the height of

"Naturaleza y origen de la confirmación *ex certa scientia,*" *Ius Canonicum* 25 (1985): 91–116.

[104] *Acta Apostolicae Sedis*, vol. 92 (2000): 765.

[105] See, for example, the approval appended to the CDF Instruction *Ardens Felicitatis* (2000), issued in the same year as *Dominus Iesus*.

[106] See Secretariat of State, *Regolamento Generale della Curia Romana* (1992), a. 110, sec. 4.

the Jubilee Year ..."[107] The Italian phrase "*in forma speciale*" corresponds closely to the traditional Latin phrase "*in forma specifica*." Moreover, according to Tarcisio Bertone, then the Secretary of the CDF, the formula of approval appended to *Dominus Iesus* is no ordinary approval but indicates "special and elevated authority."[108] But there is no formula of special or elevated authority other than the approval in the specific form.

Therefore, since the declaration *Dominus Iesus*, in virtue of its approval in the specific form, must be regarded as a formal act of the pope as supreme head of the Church, and since it proposes matters of faith in a definitive way, it must be admitted that the following propositions are infallibly defined:

> *It must be firmly believed* that, in the mystery of Jesus Christ, the incarnate Son of God, who is "the way, the truth, and the life" (Jn 14:6), the full revelation of divine truth is given.[109]

> The distinction between *theological faith* and *belief* in the other religions *must be firmly held*.[110]

> The doctrine of faith *must be firmly believed* which proclaims that Jesus of Nazareth, son of Mary, and he alone, is the Son and the Word of the Father.[111]

> The doctrine of faith regarding the unicity of the salvific economy willed by the one and triune God *must be firmly*

---

[107] Pope John Paul II, Angelus Address (Oct. 1, 2000).

[108] Cited by Dunn, "The CDF's Declaration *Dominus Iesus*," 66, with reference to Bertone's address to the Press at the presentation of *Dominus Iesus*.

[109] CDF, *Dominus Iesus*, §5.

[110] CDF, *Dominus Iesus*, §7.

[111] CDF, *Dominus Iesus*, §10.

believed, at the source and center of which is the mystery of the incarnation of the Word, mediator of divine grace on the level of creation and redemption (cf. Col 1:15–20), he who recapitulates all things (cf. Eph 1:10), he "whom God has made our wisdom, our righteousness, and sanctification and redemption" (1 Cor 1:30).[112]

The truth of Jesus Christ, Son of God, Lord and only Savior, who through the event of his Incarnation, death and resurrection has brought the history of salvation to fulfilment, and which has in him its fullness and center, *must be firmly believed* as a constant element of the Church's faith.[113]

It must therefore be *firmly believed* as a truth of Catholic faith that the universal salvific will of the one and triune God is offered and accomplished once for all in the mystery of the Incarnation, death, and resurrection of the Son of God.[114]

Therefore, in connection with the unicity and universality of the salvific mediation of Jesus Christ, the unicity of the Church founded by him *must be firmly believed* as a truth of Catholic faith. Just as there is one Christ, so there exists a single body of Christ, a single bride of Christ: "a single Catholic and apostolic Church."[115]

The Catholic faithful are *required to profess* that there is an historical continuity—rooted in the apostolic succession—

---

[112] CDF, *Dominus Iesus*, §11.
[113] CDF, *Dominus Iesus*, §13.
[114] CDF, *Dominus Iesus*, §14.
[115] CDF, *Dominus Iesus*, §16.

between the Church founded by Christ and the Catholic Church.[116]

It must be *firmly believed* that "the Church, a pilgrim now on earth, is necessary for salvation: the one Christ is the mediator and the way of salvation; he is present to us in his body which is the Church. He himself explicitly asserted the necessity of faith and baptism (cf. Mk 16:16; Jn 3:5), and thereby affirmed at the same time the necessity of the Church which men enter through baptism as through a door."[117]

REPLY TO OBJECTION 1. To the first it must be said that Salaverri offers no argument in defense of this assertion, saying merely "we may suppose" that even documents approved in the specific form "have not been approved infallibly, but with a grade of authority that is lower than a definition *ex cathedra*." Such a supposition, however, seems incompatible with what he himself also says—namely, that when the pope approves documents in the specific form, he "makes these decrees his own and they must be accepted as his formal decrees."[118] For certainly the pope is able to speak infallibly in his own formal decrees.

REPLY TO OBJECTION 2. To the second it must be said that these words of Bishop Gasser are taken out of context. What he rejects here is the idea, put forward by some, that the sole subject of infallibility in the Church is the pope, who then communicates the gift of infallibility to the Church.[119] But this does not exclude

---

[116] CDF, *Dominus Iesus*, §17.

[117] CDF, *Dominus Iesus*, §20, citing *Lumen Gentium*, §14.

[118] Salaverri, *Tractatus de Ecclesia Christi*, no. 665 (trans. Baker, *Sacrae Theologiae Summa*, vol. 1B, 244).

[119] See Mansi, 52:1216 C.

that the pope could exercise his infallibility through the CDF by approval of a document in the specific form.

REPLY TO OBJECTION 3. To the third it must be said that the pope does not delegate his teaching authority to the CDF in such a way that the latter would be able to exercise this authority independently. Rather, he allows the CDF a participation in his own teaching authority through his specific approval of individual acts, making them his own.

ARTICLE 3
Whether the Pope Speaks Infallibly in *Evangelium Vitae*?

OBJECTION 1. It would seem that the pope does not speak infallibly in *Evangelium Vitae* (1995). For Cardinal Ratzinger is reported to have said: "Pope John Paul II considered making an infallible declaration against abortion and euthanasia in his latest encyclical *Evangelium Vitae*, but the idea was dropped because the teachings were considered 'so evident' in Christian faith and tradition."[120] But if the pope did not intend to speak infallibly in *Evangelium Vitae*, then he did not speak infallibly.

OBJECTION 2. Furthermore, according to Bishop Anthony Bosco: "If the pope wanted to say something was infallible, he would have used the word."[121]

OBJECTION 3. Furthermore, in order to speak infallibly, the pope must propose a doctrine of faith or morals as *definitively to be held*, as shown above. But this phrase is not used in the encyclical.

---

[120] Cited by Francis A. Sullivan, "The Doctrinal Weight of *Evangelium vitae*," *Theological Studies* 56 (1995): 562, with reference to "On File," *Origins* 24/43 (April 13, 1995), 734.

[121] Cited by Sullivan, "Doctrinal Weight," 563, with reference to the *Pittsburgh Post-Gazette* (Mar. 30, 1995), A-5.

OBJECTION 4. Furthermore, encyclical letters are organs of the ordinary papal magisterium, which is not infallible, as shown above. But *Evangelium Vitae* is an encyclical letter.

ON THE CONTRARY, according to the Vatican summary of *Evangelium Vitae*, the encyclical contains "doctrinal affirmations of very high magisterial authority, presented with particular solemnity by the supreme pontiff,"[122] which seems to indicate an exercise of the solemn (extraordinary) magisterium, which is infallible.

I ANSWER THAT, it must be said that the three essential conditions for speaking infallibly are fulfilled in *Evangelium Vitae*. In the first place, there can be no doubt that the pope speaks in his official capacity as head of the universal Church, for the encyclical letter is explicitly addressed to all bishops, priests and deacons, men and women religious, lay faithful, and all people of good will.

Secondly, when the pope declares and confirms the grave immorality of murder, abortion, and euthanasia, it is clear that his teaching regards matters of faith or morals. As Francis Sullivan says: "In order to be capable of being taught with infallibility, a moral doctrine must be either formally revealed, or so intimately connected with revealed truth as to be required for its defense or exposition. It would seem to me that the teaching of the encyclical on the immorality of murder, abortion, and euthanasia meets that requirement."[123]

Thirdly, it is required that the pope not merely teach but *define* doctrine. Now this word "define," according to the official *relatio* on papal infallibility, "signifies that the pope directly and

---

[122] Cited by Sullivan, "Doctrinal Weight," 561, with reference to "The Vatican's Summary of *Evangelium vitae*," *Origins* 24/42 (Apr. 6, 1995), 728.

[123] Sullivan, "Doctrinal Weight," 564.

conclusively pronounces his judgment about a doctrine which concerns matters of faith and morals in such a way that each one of the faithful is able to be immediately certain … of the mind of the Roman pontiff; in such a way, indeed, that one may know for certain that this or that doctrine is held to be heretical, proximate to heresy, certain or erroneous, etc., by the Roman pontiff."[124] And there are in *Evangelium Vitae* three places in which the pope *directly* and *conclusively* pronounces his sentence about doctrines that concern morals in such a way that there can be no doubt that, according to the mind of the Roman pontiff, these doctrines are to be held definitively by the whole Church.

First, on the grave immorality of murder:

> Therefore, by the authority which Christ conferred upon Peter and his successors, and in communion with the bishops of the Catholic Church, I confirm that the direct and voluntary killing of an innocent human being is always gravely immoral. This doctrine, based upon that unwritten law which man, in the light of reason, finds in his own heart (cf. Rom 2:14–15), is reaffirmed by Sacred Scripture, transmitted by the Tradition of the Church and taught by the ordinary and universal magisterium.[125]

Now when the pope explicitly states that this doctrine is affirmed by Sacred Scripture, he proposes it as being *contained in divine revelation*; and when he states that it is transmitted by the Tradition of the Church and taught by the ordinary and universal magisterium, he makes it clear that it *is to be firmly believed as such*. Hence, the doctrine is proposed as one that is to be firmly

---

[124] Mansi, 52:1316 AB.
[125] John Paul II, Encyclical Letter *Evangelium Vitae* (1995), §57.

believed as divinely revealed. It must, therefore, be admitted that this is an infallible definition of a dogma of divine and Catholic faith (*de fide credenda*).

Secondly, on the grave immorality of abortion:

> Therefore, by the authority which Christ conferred upon Peter and his successors, in communion with the bishops—who on various occasions have condemned abortion and who in the aforementioned consultation, albeit dispersed throughout the world, have shown unanimous agreement concerning this doctrine—I declare that direct abortion, that is, abortion willed as an end or as a means, always constitutes a grave moral disorder, since it is the deliberate killing of an innocent human being. This doctrine is based upon the natural law and upon the written Word of God, is transmitted by the Church's Tradition and taught by the ordinary and universal magisterium.[126]

In this case, the pope states that this doctrine is based upon (rather than affirmed by) the written Word of God, thus proposing it as being *at least closely connected to divine revelation*; and when he states that it is transmitted by the Church's Tradition and taught by the ordinary and universal magisterium, he makes it clear that it *is to be definitively held as such*. Hence, it must be admitted that this is an infallible definition of a truth of Catholic doctrine (*de fide tenenda*).

Thirdly, on the grave immorality of euthanasia:

> Taking into account these distinctions, in harmony with the magisterium of my predecessors and in communion

---

[126] John Paul II, *Evangelium Vitae*, §62.

with the bishops of the Catholic Church, I confirm that euthanasia is a grave violation of the law of God, since it is the deliberate and morally unacceptable killing of a human person. This doctrine is based upon the natural law and upon the written Word of God, is transmitted by the Church's Tradition and taught by the ordinary and universal magisterium.[127]

Here again, when the pope states that this doctrine is based upon the written Word of God, he proposes it as being *at least closely connected to divine revelation*; and when he states that it is transmitted by the Church's Tradition and taught by the ordinary and universal magisterium, he makes it clear that it is *to be definitively held as such*. Here too, therefore, we have an infallible definition of a truth of Catholic doctrine (*de fide tenenda*).

REPLY TO OBJECTION 1. To the first it must be said that "it is a bit risky to draw firm conclusions from a partial report of what was said at a press conference,"[128] as Sullivan notes. But in any case, whether or not the pope consciously intends to speak infallibly cannot be decisive, for many popes spoke infallibly long before the doctrine of papal infallibility was clearly taught or defined. Therefore, a pope could exercise the charism of infallibility without himself fully understanding that he does so. What is decisive is that the pope intends to speak *conclusively*, or *definitively*; and this intention is manifest in *Evangelium Vitae* with respect to the grave immorality of murder, abortion, and euthanasia.

REPLY TO OBJECTION 2. To the second it must be said that "even in their solemn dogmatic definitions," as Sullivan notes,

---

[127] John Paul II, *Evangelium Vitae*, §65.
[128] Sullivan, "Doctrinal Weight," 562.

"popes have not explicitly said that they were speaking infallibly. One has to judge, on other grounds, whether the conditions laid down by Vatican I for *ex cathedra* statements were fulfilled."[129]

REPLY TO OBJECTION 3. To the third it must be said that, according to the official *relatio* on papal infallibility, it is not required for the popes to use any particular phrase or formula in their *ex cathedra* definitions.[130] And as Sullivan says: "The formula which he used in this encyclical in condemning murder, abortion, and euthanasia, would seem sufficient to remove any doubt as to whether he was expressing a judgment which he, along with the bishops, wanted all Catholics to hold definitively. It is hard to see how any other interpretation would do justice to the language which he used."[131]

REPLY TO OBJECTION 4. To the fourth it must be said that, although encyclical letters are typically used as instruments of the ordinary (authentic) papal magisterium, there is nothing to prevent the pope from using an encyclical letter to promulgate a solemn definition, as Fenton shows.[132]

ARTICLE 4
Whether the Pope Speaks Infallibly
in *Ordinatio Sacerdotalis*?

OBJECTION 1. It seems that the pope does not speak infallibly in *Ordinatio Sacerdotalis* (1994). For according to Cardinal Ratzinger: "In this case, an act of the ordinary papal magisterium, in itself

---

[129] Sullivan, "Doctrinal Weight," 563.

[130] See Mansi, 52:1215 A.

[131] Sullivan, "Doctrinal Weight," 563.

[132] Joseph C. Fenton, "The Doctrinal Authority of Papal Encyclicals," *American Ecclesiastical Review* 121 (1949): 136–50, 210–20; "Infallibility," 177–98.

not infallible, witnesses to the infallibility of the teaching of a doctrine already possessed by the Church."[133] Hence, as Sullivan says: "This language comes very close to that of a solemn definition, but we are assured by Cardinal Ratzinger that it was not the intention of John Paul II to speak *ex cathedra*."[134]

OBJECTION 2. Furthermore, according to Archbishop Bertone: "It seems a pseudo-problem to wonder whether this papal act of 'confirming' a teaching of the ordinary, universal magisterium is infallible or not." For even though it is not infallible of itself, it participates in the infallibility of the ordinary and universal magisterium, "which includes the pope not as a mere bishop but as the head of the episcopal college."[135]

ON THE CONTRARY, according to Pope Benedict XVI: "Blessed Pope John Paul II stated irrevocably that the Church has received no authority for this from the Lord."[136] And again: "The late Pope John Paul II has decided infallibly and irrevocably that the Church has not the right to ordain women to the priesthood."[137]

I ANSWER THAT, it must be said that the pope speaks infallibly in *Ordinatio Sacerdotalis*, when he says: "Wherefore, in order that all doubt may be removed regarding a matter of great importance, a matter which pertains to the Church's divine constitution itself, in virtue of Our ministry of confirming the brethren (cf. Lk 22:32), We declare that the Church has no authority whatsoever

---

[133] Ratzinger, "Letter Concerning the CDF Reply."

[134] Sullivan, *Creative Fidelity*, 22.

[135] Bertone, "Magisterial Documents and Public Dissent."

[136] Pope Benedict XVI, *Homily for Chrism Mass*, April 5, 2012.

[137] Letter of Pope Benedict XVI to Bishop William Morris, cited by Morris in *Benedict, Me and the Cardinals Three: The Story of the Dismissal of Bishop Bill Morris by Pope Benedict XVI* (Adelaide: ATF Press, 2014), 179.

to confer priestly ordination on women and that this judgment is to be definitively held by all the Church's faithful."[138]

There are, as has been shown, three necessary conditions for an infallible papal definition. In the case of *Ordinatio Sacerdotalis* there can be no doubt that the first condition (on the part of the subject) is fulfilled. For Pope John Paul II explicitly addresses this apostolic letter to all the bishops of the Catholic Church and invokes his "ministry of confirming the brethren (cf. Lk 22:32)," thereby recalling the words of the Second Vatican Council, which cites the same passage of Luke's Gospel where it says that the pope is infallible when, "as the supreme shepherd and teacher of all the faithful, who confirms his brethren in their faith 22:32)," etc.[139]

With regard to the second condition (on the part of the object), the matter in question is explicitly presented as "a matter which pertains to the Church's divine constitution itself," which is necessarily a matter pertaining to faith. Confirmation of this appears in the affirmative response of the CDF to the question: "Is the teaching that the Church has no authority whatsoever to confer priestly ordination on women, which is presented in the apostolic letter *Ordinatio Sacerdotalis* [as a thing] to be held definitively, to be understood as pertaining to the deposit of faith?"[140] For a doctrine which pertains to the deposit of faith is one which is either revealed or necessarily connected to divine revelation. In either case, it falls within the scope of papal infallibility.

---

[138] Pope John Paul II, Apostolic Letter *Ordinatio Sacerdotalis* (1994), §4, with the correct plural (our/we) as per the Latin text.

[139] Vatican II, *Lumen Gentium*, §25.

[140] CDF, Response to Dubium Concerning *Ordinatio Sacerdotalis* (1995).

With regard to the third condition (on the part of the act itself), there has been some confusion over the formula employed by the pope in proposing the doctrine as "to be definitively held," since this same formula is used by the Second Vatican Council to describe the mode of infallible teaching of the ordinary and universal magisterium, whereas the mode of infallible teaching proper to the pope is described in the same place as proclaiming a doctrine "by a definitive act."[141] This has led some theologians to wonder whether the pope was exercising (or attempting to exercise) the infallibility of the ordinary and universal magisterium. But such speculation is not to the point. For, as Ansgar Santogrossi shows,[142] the declaration of *Ordinatio Sacerdotalis* is a proper exercise of papal infallibility in its own right, as can be proved in two ways.

First, from the words of Gasser's *relatio* on papal infallibility, for the very property and note of a definition in the proper sense is "the manifest intention of defining doctrine, either of putting an end to doubt (*fluctuationi finem imponendi*) about a certain doctrine or of defining a thing by giving a definitive judgment (*definitivam sententiam*) and proposing that doctrine as one which must be held (*tenendam*) by the universal Church."[143] And this intention is manifest in *Ordinatio Sacerdotalis*. For Pope John Paul II expressly intends to remove all doubt, saying: "Wherefore, in order that all doubt may be removed." And he does so by proposing his judgment (*sententia*) as "definitively to be held (*definitive tenendam*) by all the Church's faithful."[144]

---

[141] Vatican II, *Lumen Gentium*, §25.

[142] Ansgar Santogrossi, "*Ordinatio Sacerdotalis*: A definition *ex cathedra*," *Homiletic and Pastoral Review* (Feb. 1999): 7–14.

[143] Mansi, 52:1225 C.

[144] John Paul II, *Ordinatio Sacerdotalis*, §4.

Second, it is indisputable that the bishops dispersed through-out the world would teach infallibly if they proposed the very same doctrine in the very same manner—namely, as a judgment to be definitively held by all the faithful. For according to the Second Vatican Council, the bishops "dispersed through the world, but still maintaining the bond of communion among themselves and with the successor of Peter," are infallible when "authenti-cally teaching matters of faith and morals, they are in agreement on one position (*sententiam*) as definitively to be held (*definitive tenendam*)."[145] But if one were to deny that the pope also speaks infallibly when he, as head of the Church, proposes his judgment (*sententia*) in a matter of faith or morals as definitively to be held (*definitive tenendam*), then one would fall into the error of the Gallicans, according to which the bishops have a greater teaching authority than the pope, contrary to the solemnly defined teaching of Vatican I that the pope possesses the fullness of the supreme power of jurisdiction over the universal Church, which includes the power of the magisterium.[146] Hence, it must be admitted that the pope speaks infallibly in *Ordinatio Sacerdotalis*.

REPLY TO OBJECTION 1. To the first it must be said that the private opinion of Cardinal Ratzinger is not decisive. Nor is the question of whether or not Pope John Paul II consciously under-stood himself to be speaking *ex cathedra*. The decisive question is only whether he intended to speak *definitively*, that is, *conclusively*, on a matter of faith or morals, for the whole Church. And this must be judged in light of the intention expressed in the text itself, and not by the private opinions of the pope's friends or advisors, no matter how well informed they may be of his private

---

[145] Vatican II, *Lumen Gentium*, §25.

[146] See Vatican I, *Pastor Aeternus*, ch. 3.

thoughts and intentions. Moreover, Ratzinger's assertion appears to be based on the assumption that the pope can speak infallibly only when he defines a new dogma (or doctrine), which is false, as shown above (Q. 1, a. 4).

REPLY TO OBJECTION 2. To the second it must be said that it is not a pseudo-problem, but an important question, to ask whether the act by which a pope confirms a teaching of the ordinary and universal magisterium is infallible or not. For in the absence of a solemn definition, doubt may arise as to whether a doctrine has in fact been definitively taught by the ordinary and universal magisterium, and this indeed has happened with regard to the question of women's ordination. In such a case, an infallible act of confirmation would remove all grounds for doubt about the truth of the doctrine. But if the act of confirmation were not infallible of itself, then the definitive status of the doctrine would still rest on the teaching of the ordinary and universal magisterium, which was precisely the point under dispute, and so the doubts of many would not be effectively resolved.

ARTICLE 5
Whether the Pope Speaks Infallibly in *Veritatis Splendor*?

OBJECTION 1. It seems that the pope does not speak infallibly in *Veritatis Splendor* (1993). For according to Archbishop Bertone: "In the Encyclicals *Veritatis Splendor* and *Evangelium Vitae* and in the Apostolic Letter *Ordinatio Sacerdotalis*, the Roman pontiff intended, though not in a solemn way, to confirm and reaffirm doctrines which belong to the ordinary, universal teaching of the magisterium, and which therefore are to be held in a definitive and irrevocable way." And again: "These documents deal with teachings not proposed or confirmed by the magisterium in the form of a definition (solemn judgement)."[147] But if the teaching of *Veritatis Splendor* is not proposed in a solemn way, in the form of a definition or solemn judgment, then it is not proposed infallibly, as shown above.

OBJECTION 2. Furthermore, if *Veritatis Splendor* contained *ex cathedra* teaching, there would be at least some reputable Catholic theologians maintaining this thesis; but there seem to be none.

ON THE CONTRARY, Bertone errs in denying the infallibility of *Evangelium Vitae* and *Ordinatio Sacerdotalis*, as shown above. Therefore, it is likely that he also errs in denying the infallibility of *Veritatis Splendor*, since, according to his own words, Pope John Paul II intended, in each of these three cases, "to confirm and reaffirm doctrines which belong to the ordinary, universal teaching of the magisterium, and which therefore are to be held in a definitive and irrevocable way."[148]

I ANSWER THAT, it must be said that Pope John Paul II speaks infallibly on the central doctrine of this encyclical letter, which is "the reaffirmation of the universality and immutability of the moral commandments, particularly those which prohibit always and without exception intrinsically evil acts."[149] This can be seen from an examination of the three essential conditions for papal infallibility.

First, on the part of the subject, the pope explicitly appeals to his ministry of confirming his brethren (cf. Lk 22:32) and invokes his apostolic authority, saying: "Each of us knows how important is the teaching which represents the central theme of

---

[147] Bertone, "Magisterial Documents."
[148] Ibid.
[149] Pope John Paul II, Encyclical Letter *Veritatis Splendor* (1993), §115.

this encyclical and which is today being restated with the authority of the Successor of Peter."[150]

Second, on the part of the object, John Paul II presents this central teaching as a moral doctrine intimately connected to divine revelation, saying: "In teaching the existence of intrinsically evil acts, the Church accepts the teaching of Sacred Scripture. The Apostle Paul emphatically states: 'Do not be deceived: neither the immoral, nor idolaters, nor adulterers, nor sexual perverts, nor thieves, nor the greedy, nor drunkards, nor revilers, nor robbers will inherit the Kingdom of God' (1 Cor 6:9–10)."[151]

Third, on the part of the act, the reaffirmation of the existence of intrinsically evil acts is expressed in the encyclical letter as follows:

> *One must therefore reject the thesis*, characteristic of teleological and proportionalist theories, *which holds that it is impossible to qualify as morally evil according to its species*—its "object"—*the deliberate choice of certain kinds of behavior or specific acts, apart from a consideration of the intention for which the choice is made or the totality of the foreseeable consequences of that act for all persons concerned.*[152]

And again:

> For this reason—we repeat—the opinion must be rejected as erroneous which maintains that it is impossible to qualify as morally evil according to its species the deliberate choice of certain kinds of behavior or specific acts, without taking into account the intention for which the choice was made

---

[150] John Paul II, *Veritatis Splendor*, §115.
[151] John Paul II, *Veritatis Splendor*, §81.
[152] John Paul II, *Veritatis Splendor*, §79, emphasis in original.

or the totality of the foreseeable consequences of that act for all persons concerned.[153]

By these words the pope not only reaffirms the existence of intrinsically evil acts, but proclaims this doctrine by a definitive act. In the first place, the pope repeats his central condemnation twice in the space of four paragraphs, which is highly unusual and cannot but give added force to the condemnation, for the frequent repetition of a doctrine is one of the notes by which the degree of authority of papal statements is to be judged, as the Second Vatican Council teaches.[154] Secondly, the pope qualifies the condemned opinion as "erroneous" (*ut erronea*), which, in the traditional terminology of theological censures, is the negative equivalent of a theologically certain truth of Catholic doctrine, just as "heretical" is the negative equivalent of a dogma to be believed by divine and Catholic faith. Finally, the pope declares that this erroneous proposition "must be rejected" (*respuenda est*), thus expressing the obligatory nature of the condemnation. For to say that a proposition "must be rejected as erroneous" is equivalent to saying that the opposing truth "must be held as true," which is the same as proposing that truth as one that is definitively to be held. And this is the essential note of definition, as shown above (Q. 1, a. 1).

REPLY TO OBJECTION 1. To the first it must be said that Bertone's opinion appears to be based on the assumption that the pope can speak infallibly only when he defines a new dogma (or doctrine), which is false, as shown above (Q. 1, a. 4).

REPLY TO OBJECTION 2. To the second it must be said that this objection would have more weight were it not for the fact

[153] John Paul II, *Veritatis Splendor*, §82.
[154] Ibid.

that this encyclical was published at a time when most Catholic theologians routinely denied the infallibility of all but the most solemn dogmatic definitions. In such a context it is unsurprising that very little consideration has been given to the question of infallible teaching in *Veritatis Splendor*.

ARTICLE 6
Whether the *Credo* of Paul VI Is an Infallible Profession of Faith?

OBJECTION 1. It seems that the *Credo of the People of God* of Paul VI (1968) is an infallible profession of faith. For it was issued by Pope Paul VI, in fulfillment of "the mandate entrusted by Christ to Peter ... to confirm our brothers in the faith."[155] And the profession of faith is a pre-eminent form of infallible definition. For as St. Thomas says: "To publish a new edition of the symbol belongs to that authority which is empowered to decide matters of faith finally (*sententialiter determinare*), so that they may be held by all with unshaken faith. Now this belongs to the authority of the Sovereign Pontiff."[156]

OBJECTION 2. Furthermore, Pope Paul VI introduces his profession of faith, saying: "Today We are offered the opportunity of declaring Our judgment (*sententia*) in a more solemn mode (*sollemniore modo*)."[157] But the solemn judgments of the pope are infallible.

ON THE CONTRARY, the pope himself says in the preamble to this creed that it is "not, strictly speaking, a dogmatic definition."[158]

---

[155] Pope Paul VI, *Solemni Hac Liturgia* (1968), §3.
[156] Thomas Aquinas, *Summa Theologiae* II-II, q. 1, a. 10.
[157] Paul VI, *Solemni Hac Liturgia*, §6.
[158] Paul VI, *Solemni Hac Liturgia*, §3.

I ANSWER THAT, it must be said that the *Credo* of Paul VI would certainly qualify as an infallible profession of faith were it not for the substantial element of doubt introduced by his own qualification when he says, in the introductory part of the text itself, that this creed is "not, strictly speaking, a dogmatic definition." It may be objected that by these words the pope denies only that this creed is *dogmatic* and not that it is *definitive*, thus leaving open the possibility that it is an infallible definition of doctrine (*de fide tenenda*). But against this is the consistent use of the term "*credimus*" ("we believe"), which is the language of properly dogmatic professions of faith, rather than *tenemus* ("we hold"), which would indicate a merely doctrinal definition. Moreover, the contents of the creed, which "repeats in substance ... the creed of Nicaea,"[159] is evidently dogmatic and not merely doctrinal.

Hence it seems more probable that these words manifest a deliberate intention on the part of Paul VI to downgrade the authority of his profession of faith out of a fear that, if he "were to have the air of *prescribing* or *imposing* his profession of faith in the name of his Magisterium, either he would have to tell the whole truth, raising a storm, or would have to take precautions, avoiding dealing with the more dangerously threatened points, and that would be the worst thing of all."[160] This casts substantial doubt on the infallibility of Paul VI's profession of faith; and according to the *Code of Canon Law*: "No doctrine is understood to be defined infallibly unless this is manifestly evident."[161]

From this the replies to the objections should be clear.

---

[159] Paul VI, *Solemni Hac Liturgia*, §3.

[160] Interview with Cardinal Georges Cottier by Gianni Valente, "Paul VI, Maritain and the Faith of the Apostles," *30 Days*, no. 4 (2008).

[161] CIC, 749, §3.

ARTICLE 7
Whether the Pope Speaks Infallibly in *Humanae Vitae*?

OBJECTION 1. It seems that the pope does not speak infallibly in *Humanae Vitae* (1968). For the infallibility of the Church does not extend beyond matters of faith and morals that are directly contained in divine revelation or that are required for safeguarding and expounding the same. But the prohibition of artificial birth control is a specific moral norm of natural law that does not appear to be directly revealed, nor is it strictly necessary for safeguarding and expounding divine revelation.[162] Therefore, this doctrine cannot be taught infallibly.

OBJECTION 2. Furthermore, according to the remarks of Ferdinando Lambruschini in his presentation of the encyclical at the Vatican press conference, its teaching is not infallible.

OBJECTION 3. Furthermore, none of the customary phrases by which the popes have traditionally signaled their intention to define a doctrine are present in *Humanae Vitae*.

OBJECTION 4. Furthermore, according to the *Code of Canon Law*: "No doctrine is understood to be defined infallibly unless this is manifestly evident."[163] Now if it were manifestly evident that the pope was speaking infallibly in *Humanae Vitae*, this would be recognized by a consensus of Catholic theologians.[164] But in fact most Catholic theologians do not regard the teaching of *Humanae Vitae* as infallible.[165]

---

[162] See Sullivan, *Magisterium*, 148–52.

[163] 1983 *CIC*, can. 749, §3.

[164] See Francis A. Sullivan, "The 'Secondary Object' of Infallibility," *Theological Studies* 54 (1993): 548–49.

[165] See Sullivan, *Magisterium*, 152.

ON THE CONTRARY, according to Ermenegildo Lio, in his book *Humanae Vitae e Infallibilità,* for which he received a personal letter of thanks from Pope John Paul II, *Humanae Vitae* contains a solemn *ex cathedra* definition of the intrinsic immorality of artificial birth control.[166]

I ANSWER THAT, it must be said that the condemnation of artificial methods of birth control in *Humanae Vitae* fulfills the three essential criteria set forth by Vatican I for the exercise of papal infallibility. In the first place, there can be no doubt that the pope is exercising his office of pastor and teacher of all Christians. For the encyclical is addressed "to his venerable brothers the patriarchs, archbishops, bishops and other local ordinaries in peace and communion with the Apostolic See, to the clergy and faithful of the whole Catholic world, and to all men of good will."[167] Moreover, the pope explicitly declares that he speaks "in virtue of the mandate entrusted to us by Christ."[168]

Second, as regards the object of papal infallibility, the teaching of the encyclical is presented as "a teaching which is based on the natural law as illuminated and enriched by divine revelation."[169] Here there is some question as to whether this moral doctrine is contained at least within the secondary object of infallibility. That it is can be proved in two ways.

In one way, the argument proceeds from the positive assertion that the authority of the Church's magisterium extends to the whole natural law, as Paul VI says: "No member of the faithful

---

[166] Ermenegildo Lio, *Humanae Vitae e Infallibilità: il Concilio, Paolo VI e Giovanni Paolo II* (Vatican City: Libreria Editrice Vaticana, 1986).

[167] Pope Paul VI, Encyclical Letter *Humanae Vitae* (1968).

[168] Paul VI, *Humanae Vitae,* §6.

[169] Paul VI, *Humanae Vitae,* §4.

could possibly deny that the Church is competent in her magisterium to interpret the natural moral law."[170] But the infallibility of the Church extends as far as her magisterium itself extends. The object of the authentic magisterium in general, and of the infallible magisterium in particular, are described in precisely the same way as "matters of faith and morals." For the Second Vatican Council says: "In matters of faith and morals, the bishops speak in the name of Christ and the faithful are to accept their teaching and adhere to it with a religious assent," and this pertains to the authentic magisterium. In the same place, the object of the infallible teaching of the ordinary and universal magisterium is described as "matters of faith and morals." And again, the object of infallible papal teaching is also said to be "doctrine of faith or morals." These identical descriptions are due to the fact that the infallible magisterium and the merely authentic (non-definitive) magisterium are not distinguished by their *object*, but by their *mode of teaching*. For the former is proclaimed "by a definitive act,"[171] whereas in the latter case, the pope or the college of bishops "do not intend to proclaim these teachings by a definitive act."[172]

In another way, the argument proceeds from the close connection of the natural law to the ultimate purpose of divine revelation. For the secondary object of the Church's infallibility extends to every truth that is "intimately connected" to divine revelation,[173] whether more or less strictly, as Gasser says: "Together with revealed truths, there are other truths more or less strictly connected. These truths, although they are not revealed in themselves, are

---

[170] Paul VI, *Humanae Vitae*, §4.

[171] All cited from Vatican II, *Lumen Gentium*, §25.

[172] CDF, *Professio Fidei* (1998).

[173] CDF, *Donum Veritatis*, §16.

nevertheless required in order to guard fully, explain properly, and define efficaciously the very deposit of faith."[174] Now the truth concerning particular moral norms of the natural law is necessarily connected with divine revelation on account of the ultimate purpose of divine revelation, which is man's salvation. For as Paul VI says: "The natural law, too, declares the will of God, and its faithful observance is necessary for men's eternal salvation."[175] And again, according to Pope Pius XI: "Every human action has a necessary connection with man's last end, and therefore cannot be withdrawn from the dictates of the divine law, of which the Church is guardian, interpreter, and infallible mistress."[176] The infallibility of the Church, therefore, extends to the whole range of human actions insofar as they are intrinsically good or evil, whether on account of the law revealed by God or on account of the law written by God upon the human heart.

The third essential condition for the exercise of papal infallibility is the note of definition, which appears when the pope "directly and conclusively pronounces his judgment" (*suam sententiam directe et terminative proferat*) concerning faith or morals.[177] Now in the condemnation of artificial methods of birth control at the heart of *Humanae Vitae*, the pope directly and conclusively pronounces his sentence with the manifest intention of putting an end to doubt about this question. For the pope declares that withdrawal, abortion, sterilization, and contraception must be rejected (*respuendum est*) and condemned (*damnandum est*) absolutely (*omnino*), thus manifestly intending to oblige the faithful to

---

[174] Mansi, 52:1226 B.
[175] Paul VI, *Humanae Vitae*, §4.
[176] Pope Pius XI, *Divini Illius Magistri* (1929), §18.
[177] Mansi, 52:1316 B.

give a firm and unqualified assent to the doctrine of the intrinsic immorality of these acts.

For he says first:

> Therefore, relying on these first principles of a human and Christian doctrine of marriage, We must once more declare that the direct interruption of the generative process already begun and, above all, all direct abortion, even for therapeutic reasons, are to be absolutely rejected (*omnino respuendam esse*) as lawful means of regulating the number of children.[178]

Then he adds:

> Equally to be condemned (*Pariter damnandum est*), as the magisterium of the Church has many times taught, is direct sterilization, whether of the man or of the woman, whether permanent or temporary.[179]

And then again:

> Similarly to be rejected (*Item respuendus est*) is any action before, during, or after sexual intercourse, that is specifically intended to prevent procreation, whether as an end or as a means.[180]

Therefore, since it is the same thing to say that these acts *must be absolutely rejected and condemned* as unlawful and to say that their intrinsic immorality *must be definitively held*, it must be concluded that these condemnations manifest the essential note

---

[178] Paul VI, *Humanae Vitae*, §14.
[179] Paul VI, *Humanae Vitae*, §14.
[180] Paul VI, *Humanae Vitae*, §14.

of definition, and hence that *Humanae Vitae* contains infallible papal teaching.

REPLY TO OBJECTION 1. To the first it must be said that specific moral norms of the natural law fall at least within the secondary object of infallibility on account of their necessity for salvation, which is the ultimate purpose of divine revelation, as said above. Moreover, this objection would undermine the whole doctrine of papal infallibility. For if it were admissible for anyone to judge that the pope does not speak infallibly in a certain instance because the doctrine proposed does not, according to his own opinion, pertain to the deposit of faith, then it would be possible to assert that any papal definition, such as even that of the Immaculate Conception or the Assumption of Mary, is not infallible because, according to his own opinion, the doctrine in question is neither contained in divine revelation nor is it required for the safeguarding and exposition of the deposit of the same. But this is absurd. Rather, as Jean-Marie Hervé notes:

> It is also up to the Church to decide how far her infallibility extends: otherwise there could never be any certainty as to whether, in defining something, she had transgressed the limits of her magisterium. In that case infallibility would be placed in grave peril, and the whole of religion would turn out to be placed in doubt. From this it follows that, if the Church declares that something pertains to her magisterium, or proposes it as requiring the assent of faith, such a decree is to be held as infallible.[181]

---

[181] Cited by Brian W. Harrison, "The *Ex Cathedra* Status of the Encyclical *Humanae Vitae*," *Living Tradition* 43 (Sep.–Nov., 1992), with reference to Jean-Marie Hervé, *Manuale theologiae dogmaticae*, vol. 1 (Paris: Berche & Pagis, 1935), 507.

What is necessary to determine with regard to the object of papal infallibility, therefore, is not whether the doctrine taught is *in fact* a matter of faith or morals, but whether it is being *proposed as such*.

REPLY TO OBJECTION 2. To the second it must be said that this represents no more than the personal opinion of Lambruschini. Moreover, this aspect of his remarks was erased from the official account of the press conference, which appeared the next day in *L'Osservatore Romano*.[182]

REPLY TO OBJECTION 3. To the third it must be said that the popes who have reigned over the Church since the Second Vatican Council, which inaugurated an era of heightened emphasis on collegiality and ecumenism, have tended to avoid the more solemn-sounding formulae in their teaching. Such solemn formulae, however, although generally sufficient to indicate infallible teaching, are not strictly necessary (see Q. 1, a. 7).

REPLY TO OBJECTION 4. To the fourth it must be said that, although the consensus of Catholic theologians may be sufficient, it is not necessary for manifesting the fact of an infallible definition. As Brian Harrison notes: "Such an interpretation of the code would in effect give the theological 'establishment' at any given period a kind of veto power over the Roman pontiff himself," which is absurd. On the contrary, "it is 'manifestly the case' that a certain doctrine is infallibly defined whenever it emerges plainly and clearly from the words of the relevant documents that there was an intention of giving a certain, final, decisive judgment on a point of faith or morals to be held by the universal Church."[183]

---

[182] See *L'Osservatore Romano* (Italian), July 29/30, 1968.
[183] Harrison, "*Ex Cathedra* Status of the Encyclical *Humanae Vitae*."

ARTICLE 8
Whether the "Oath against Modernism" Is an Infallible Profession of Faith?

OBJECTION 1. It seems that the Oath against Modernism (1910) is not an infallible profession of faith. For Sixtus Cartechini attributes this oath to the ordinary papal magisterium,[184] which is not infallible, as shown above (Q. 1, a. 2).

OBJECTION 2. Furthermore, the Oath against Modernism was abrogated in 1967 and replaced by a very brief profession of faith composed by the CDF.[185] Hence it must have been only a provisional disciplinary measure and not an irrevocable definition of faith.

ON THE CONTRARY, according to St. Thomas: "To publish a new edition of the symbol belongs to that authority which is empowered to decide matters of faith finally (*sententialiter determinare*), so that they may be held by all with unshaken faith. Now this belongs to the authority of the Sovereign Pontiff."[186] The pope, therefore, is infallible in publishing new editions of the creed or professions of faith, and the Oath against Modernism is such a profession of faith.

I ANSWER THAT, it must be said that the Oath against Modernism is a solemn and infallible profession of faith that was proposed as a binding rule of faith for the whole Church. This can be proved in two ways.

---

[184] Sixtus Cartechini, *De valore notarum theologicarum* (Rome, 1951), 34.

[185] CDF, Formula to adopt from now on in cases in which the Profession of Faith is prescribed by law in substitution of the Tridentine formula and the Oath against Modernism (1967).

[186] Thomas Aquinas, ST II-II, q. 1, a. 10.

First, positively: the oath fulfills the three essential criteria of infallible papal teaching set forth by Vatican I. For it was promulgated by Pope Pius X acting in his official capacity as supreme head of the whole Church and invoking his apostolic duty to "confirm the brethren" (cf. Luke 22:32).[187] Its object is the profession and defense of the Catholic faith against errors that would undermine the integrity of the divine deposit, on account of which it falls at least within the secondary object of infallibility. Finally, the note of definition is evident in the very language of the oath, which says: "I firmly embrace and accept.... I profess.... I believe with equally firm faith.... I hold with certainty and sincerely confess.... I also reject the error.... I condemn and reject.... Finally, I profess.... Thus I hold steadfastly.... I promise that I shall keep all this faithfully, wholly, and sincerely...."[188]

Second, speculatively: for if it were possible for such an oath to contain error in matters of faith, then it would be possible for the entire hierarchy of the Church to fall away from the true faith, for all Catholic bishops and priests were required to swear this oath for many years (1910–1967). But this is contrary to the indefectibility of the Church, according to the words of Christ: "The gates of hell shall not prevail against it" (Matt 16:18).

REPLY TO OBJECTION 1. To the first it must be said that Cartechini affirmed the infallibility of the Oath against Modernism even while attributing it to the ordinary papal magisterium. This is because he held that the pope was able to speak infallibly both in his ordinary and extraordinary magisterium, and so regarded

---

[187] See Joseph C. Fenton, "*Sacrorum Antistitum* and the Background of the Oath against Modernism," *American Ecclesiastical Review* 143 (1960): 240.

[188] Pope Pius X, *Sacrorum Antistitum* (1910).

the distinction between these two forms of teaching as a question of minor significance.[189]

REPLY TO OBJECTION 2. To the second it must be said that a distinction must be made between the oath in itself and the mandate requiring it to be sworn by bishops, pastors, professors of theology and philosophy, etc. The latter is indeed merely disciplinary, but the oath in itself is a solemn profession of faith that remains permanently valid, just as the Tridentine profession of faith remains one of the most solemn and venerable creeds of the Church despite no longer being imposed by canon law in the way that it was for over four hundred years.

ARTICLE 9
Whether the Pope Speaks Infallibly in *Quanta Cura*?

OBJECTION 1. It seems that the pope does not speak infallibly in *Quanta Cura* (1864). For the errors condemned therein are not condemned specifically as heretical. And as Sullivan says: "Since this form of censure does not explicitly condemn any particular proposition as heretical, one cannot conclude that the contradictory of any of the condemned propositions is a defined dogma. Such documents, therefore, are to be seen as examples of the ordinary, non-definitive exercise of the papal magisterium."[190]

OBJECTION 2. Furthermore, according to Robert Miller: "Pius IX taught *ex cathedra* in his bull *Ineffabilis Deus* (1854) defining the dogma of the Immaculate Conception, and *Quanta Cura* is nothing like *Ineffabilis Deus*."[191]

---

[189] See Cartechini, *De valore*, 33–36.

[190] Sullivan, *Creative Fidelity*, 89.

[191] Robert T. Miller, "Integralism and Catholic Doctrine," *Public Discourse*, July 15, 2018.

OBJECTION 3. Furthermore, as Miller also says, the doctrine contained in *Quanta Cura* cannot be taught infallibly, for it is not contained in natural law, nor in Scripture, nor in Tradition.[192]

ON THE CONTRARY, Billot includes *Quanta Cura* in his list of *ex cathedra* definitions.[193]

I ANSWER THAT, it must be said that the pope indeed speaks infallibly in *Quanta Cura* when he condemns several "false and perverse opinions" characteristic of the modern age in the following terms:

> Amidst, therefore, such great perversity of depraved opinions, we, well remembering our Apostolic office, and very greatly solicitous for our most holy religion, for sound doctrine and the salvation of souls which is entrusted to us by God, and also for the welfare of human society itself, have thought it right again to raise up our Apostolic voice. Therefore, by our Apostolic authority, we reprobate, proscribe, and condemn each and every one of the perverse opinions and doctrines individually mentioned in this letter, and we will and command that they be held by all children of the Catholic Church as absolutely reprobated, proscribed and condemned.[194]

In the first place, there can be no doubt that the pope is here exercising his supreme apostolic authority, which he explicitly invokes.

Second, it can be seen that the doctrines condemned in *Quanta Cura* fall within the scope of infallibility from the reason the pope gives for their condemnation, namely: "because they chiefly tend

---

[192] Miller, "Integralism and Catholic Doctrine."
[193] See Billot, *Tractatus de Ecclesia Christi*, 644.
[194] Pope Pius IX, Encyclical Letter *Quanta Cura* (1864), §6.

to this, that that salutary influence be impeded and even removed, which the Catholic Church, according to the institution and command of her divine Author, should freely exercise even to the end of the world—not only over private individuals, but over nations, peoples, and their sovereign princes."[195] For infallibility extends as far as is required for the safeguarding and exposition of divine revelation, which certainly includes the institutions and commands of Christ.

Third, the note of definition is manifest in the whole formula of condemnation, and especially in this, that all the faithful are explicitly obliged to hold these opinions "as absolutely rejected, proscribed, and condemned (*veluti reprobatas, proscriptas atque damnatas omnino*)."[196]

The errors thus infallibly condemned in *Quanta Cura* are as follows:

> That the best constitution of public society and also civil progress altogether require that human society be conducted and governed without regard being had to religion any more than if it did not exist; or, at least, without any distinction being made between the true religion and false ones.

> That the best condition of civil society is one in which no duty is recognized, as attached to the civil power, of restraining by enacted penalties, offenders against the Catholic religion, except so far as public peace may require.

> That liberty of conscience and worship is each man's personal right, which ought to be legally proclaimed and asserted in every rightly constituted society.

[195] Pius IX, *Quanta Cura*, §3.
[196] Pius IX, *Quanta Cura*, §6.

That a right resides in the citizens to an absolute liberty, which should be restrained by no authority whether ecclesiastical or civil, whereby they may be able openly and publicly to manifest and declare any of their ideas whatever, either by word of mouth, by the press, or in any other way.[197]

That the people's will, manifested by what is called public opinion or in some other way, constitutes a supreme law, free from all divine and human control.[198]

That in the political order accomplished facts, from the very circumstance that they are accomplished, have the force of right.

That permission should be refused to citizens and to the Church, whereby they may openly give alms for the sake of Christian charity.

That the law should be abrogated whereby on certain fixed days servile works are prohibited because of God's worship.

That domestic society or the family derives the whole principle of its existence from the civil law alone.

That on civil law alone depend all rights of parents over their children, and especially that of providing for education.

That the clergy, as being hostile to the true and beneficial advance of science and civilization, should be removed from the whole charge and duty of instructing and educating youth.

---

[197] All cited from Pius IX, *Quanta Cura*, §3.
[198] All cited from Pius IX, *Quanta Cura*, §4.

That the Church's laws do not bind in conscience unless when they are promulgated by the civil power.

That acts and decrees of the Roman Pontiffs, referring to religion and the Church, need the civil power's sanction and approbation, or at least its consent.

That the Apostolic Constitutions, whereby secret societies are condemned (whether an oath of secrecy be or be not required in such societies), and whereby their frequenters and favorers are smitten with anathema, have no force in those regions of the world wherein associations of the kind are tolerated by the civil government.

That the excommunication pronounced by the Council of Trent and by Roman Pontiffs against those who assail and usurp the Church's rights and possessions, rests on a confusion between the spiritual and temporal orders, and is directed to the pursuit of a purely secular good.

That the Church can decree nothing which binds the conscience of the faithful in regard to their use of temporal things.

That the Church has no right of restraining by temporal punishments those who violate her laws.

That it is conformable to the principles of sacred theology and public law to assert and claim for the civil government a right of property in those goods which are possessed by the Church, by the Religious Orders, and by other pious establishments.

That ecclesiastical power is not by divine right distinct from, and independent of, the civil power, and such distinction and independence cannot be preserved without the civil power's essential rights being assailed and usurped by the Church.

That without sin and without any sacrifice of the Catholic profession, assent and obedience may be refused to those judgments and decrees of the Apostolic See, whose object is declared to concern the Church's general good and her rights and discipline, so only it does not touch the dogmata of faith and morals.[199]

REPLY TO OBJECTION 1. To the first it must be said that the objection assumes that the infallibility of the pope is limited to the primary object of the magisterium, which is false, as shown above (Q. 1, a. 5).

REPLY TO OBJECTION 2. To the second it must be said that it is irrelevant whether *Quanta Cura* measures up to the standard of a dogmatic definition like *Ineffabilis Deus*; what is required is that it should meet the conditions for infallible papal teaching set forth by *Pastor Aeternus* and reiterated by *Lumen Gentium*. A thing can fail to measure up to the most pre-eminent example of its kind or class while still being a member of that kind or class.

REPLY TO OBJECTION 3. To the third it must be said that this objection would undermine the whole doctrine of papal infallibility. For if it were admissible for anyone to judge that the pope does not speak infallibly in a certain instance because the doctrine proposed does not, according to his own opinion, pertain to the deposit of faith, then it would be possible to deny the infallibility

---

[199] All cited from Pius IX, *Quanta Cura*, §5.

of any papal definition at all simply on the grounds that, according to one's own opinion, the doctrine in question is neither contained in divine revelation nor required for the safeguarding and exposition of the same. But this is absurd, as shown above (Q. 2, a. 7, ad 1). As Joseph Kleutgen says:

> Certainly it is true that the authority of the Church has its limits: for it has been given to teach about the religion of Jesus Christ, and not about everything that is able to be known by man. But what follows from this, if not that the Church teaches nothing and decides about nothing other than that which belongs to the religion of Jesus Christ? Were she not given the infallible insight as to how far her authority to teach reached, then her infallibility itself would obviously be void and meaningless. Thus whenever the bearer of this supreme authority judges about a teaching in such a way that he obliges the whole of Christendom to submit to his judgment, then is the certainty of this judgment beyond doubt.[200]

The criterion of matters of faith and morals is not given to us in order that we should make an independent inquiry into the sources of theology prior to accepting definitive magisterial teaching. It is given in order to assure us that God will prevent the pope from requiring us to hold by faith something that does not pertain to faith. What is necessary to determine with regard to the object of papal infallibility, therefore, as has been said above, is not whether the doctrine taught is *in fact* a matter of faith or morals, but whether it is being *proposed as such*.

---

[200] Kleutgen, *Die Theologie der Vorzeit*, 2nd ed., 150.

ARTICLE 10
Whether the Pope Speaks Infallibly
in *Providentissimus Deus*?

OBJECTION 1. It seems that the pope does not speak infallibly in *Providentissimus Deus* (1893). For if there were any infallible teaching in *Providentissimus Deus*, it would be the teaching concerning the complete inspiration and inerrancy of Scripture. But according to Dublanchy, this belongs to the ordinary papal magisterium,[201] which is not infallible, as shown above (Q. 1, a. 3).

OBJECTION 2. Furthermore, in order to speak infallibly, the pope must be speaking in virtue of his supreme apostolic authority as head of the universal Church. But this encyclical is not addressed to the universal Church. For the universal Church includes the lay faithful, whereas this encyclical is addressed only: "To our venerable brethren, all patriarchs, primates, archbishops, and bishops of the Catholic world, in grace and communion with the Apostolic See."[202] Nor does the pope ever invoke his supreme apostolic authority in this encyclical.

OBJECTION 3. Furthermore, the pope does not himself define Catholic doctrine concerning the inspiration and inerrancy of Scripture, but merely asserts that it has been defined by the Councils of Florence and Trent. Hence, this is an act of the ordinary (non-infallible) papal magisterium confirming or reaffirming existing Catholic doctrine.

OBJECTION 4. Furthermore, according to Cardinal König: "The Bible's references to matters of history and natural science

---

[201] See Dublanchy, "Infaillibilité," 1705.

[202] Pope Leo XIII, Encyclical Letter *Providentissimus Deus* (1893).

sometimes fall short of the truth."[203] Therefore, the teaching of *Providentissimus Deus* on the absolute inerrancy of Scripture cannot be infallible.

OBJECTION 5. Furthermore, according to the Second Vatican Council: "The books of Scripture must be acknowledged as teaching solidly, faithfully, and without error that truth which God wanted put into sacred writings for the sake of our salvation."[204] Hence, according to the *instrumentum laboris* of the 2008 synod of bishops on the Word of God in the life and mission of the Church, it can be said with certainty that "with regards to what might be inspired in the many parts of Sacred Scripture, inerrancy applies only to 'that truth which God wanted put into sacred writings for the sake of salvation.'"[205] By placing this limitation on the inerrancy of Scripture, the Second Vatican Council substantially altered the Church's previous teaching on inerrancy, as Raymond Brown says:

> In the last one hundred years we have moved from an understanding wherein inspiration guaranteed that the Bible was totally inerrant to an understanding wherein inerrancy is limited to the Bible's teaching of "that truth which God wanted put into the sacred writings for the sake of our salvation." In this long journey of thought the concept of inerrancy was not rejected but was seriously modified to fit the evidence of biblical criticism which showed that the

---

[203] *Acta Synodalia*, 3/3:275 (trans. Brian W. Harrison in "Paul VI on the Truth and Inerrancy of Sacred Scripture: Part B," *Living Tradition* 166 [2013]: 3).

[204] Vatican II, *Dei Verbum*, §11.

[205] Synod of Bishops XII Ordinary General Assembly, *Instrumentum Laboris* (2008), 15.

Bible was not inerrant in questions of science, of history, and even of time-conditioned religious beliefs.[206]

But such a substantial modification of doctrine would not have been possible if Leo XIII's teaching had been infallible.

ON THE CONTRARY, according to Pope Benedict XV, Pope Leo XIII "solemnly declared the ancient and traditional belief of the Church touching the absolute immunity of Scripture from error."[207] And again: "These words of our predecessor leave no room for doubt or dispute."[208] Likewise, Pius XII remarks on "this teaching, which Our Predecessor Leo XIII set forth with such solemnity."[209] But a solemn declaration that excludes all doubt can only be an infallible definition.

I ANSWER THAT, it must be said that Pope Leo XIII infallibly defined the complete inspiration and inerrancy of Scripture, where he says:

> But it is absolutely wrong and forbidden, either to narrow inspiration to certain parts only of Holy Scripture, or to admit that the sacred writer has erred. For the system of those who, in order to rid themselves of these difficulties, do not hesitate to concede that divine inspiration regards the things of faith and morals, and nothing beyond, because (as they wrongly think) in a question of the truth or falsehood of a passage, we should consider not so much what God has said as the reason and purpose which He had in

---

[206] Raymond E. Brown, *The Virginal Conception and Bodily Resurrection of Jesus* (New York: Paulist, 1973), 8–9.

[207] Pope Benedict XV, Encyclical Letter *Spiritus Paraclitus* (1920), §16.

[208] Benedict XV, *Spiritus Paraclitus*, §18.

[209] Pope Pius XII, Encyclical Letter *Divino Afflante Spiritu* (1943), §4.

mind in saying it—this system cannot be tolerated. For all the books which the Church receives as sacred and canonical, are written wholly and entirely, with all their parts, at the dictation of the Holy Ghost; and so far is it from being possible that any error can co-exist with inspiration, that inspiration not only is essentially incompatible with error, but excludes and rejects it as absolutely and necessarily as it is impossible that God Himself, the supreme Truth, can utter that which is not true. This is the ancient and unchanging faith of the Church, solemnly defined in the Councils of Florence and of Trent, and finally confirmed and more expressly formulated by the Council of the Vatican.[210]

In the first place, there can be no doubt that the inspiration and truth of Scripture are matters pertaining to faith. Moreover, the entire encyclical is an act of the pope in his official capacity as supreme pastor and teacher of the universal Church, for it is addressed directly and explicitly to the entire Catholic hierarchy, and therefore also indirectly and implicitly to all the faithful subject to them.

The only question to arise regards the note of definition, whether the pope proposes this teaching as to be *firmly* believed or *definitively* held; and it must be said that he does. For he *directly* and *conclusively* issues his sentence in order to *definitively exclude* a novel doctrine then being put forward by some, saying: "It is *absolutely* wrong" to limit the inspiration or inerrancy of Scripture. Moreover, the word here translated as "wrong" is *nefas*, which literally means "contrary to divine law." The pope

---

[210] Leo XIII, *Providentissimus Deus*, 20.

therefore declares that it is *absolutely contrary to divine law* to deny the complete inspiration and inerrancy of Scripture. And this is why the system of those who attempt to limit the inspiration of Scripture "must not be tolerated" (*nec toleranda est*). Furthermore, the pope concludes by expressly declaring that this doctrine of the complete inspiration and inerrancy of Scripture "is the ancient and unchanging faith of the Church, solemnly defined in the Councils of Florence and of Trent," etc., which leaves no room for doubt that, according to the mind of the Roman pontiff, the contrary opinion is to be held as heretical or at least proximate to heresy.

REPLY TO OBJECTION 1. To this it must be said that Dublanchy affirmed the infallibility of this declaration even while attributing it to the ordinary papal magisterium. This is because he held that the pope was able to speak infallibly both in his ordinary and extraordinary magisterium, distinguishing between them only on the basis of extrinsic solemnity.[211]

REPLY TO OBJECTION 2. To the second it must be said that it is not necessary for the pope to explicitly address the lay faithful in order to exercise his supreme authority; it is proof enough that he is acting as supreme head of the universal Church if he addresses the entire hierarchy of the Church, for then it is clear that he is not acting in a private capacity nor merely as the local diocesan bishop, etc. Moreover, by directly obliging all the bishops of the Church to hold and teach a certain doctrine, the pope indirectly requires all the faithful, who are subject to their bishops, to accept and hold the same teaching.

REPLY TO OBJECTION 3. To the third it must be said that there is nothing to prevent the pope from speaking infallibly when he

---

[211] See Dublanchy, "Infaillibilité," 1705.

issues a formal confirmation of existing Catholic doctrine, as has been shown above.

REPLY TO OBJECTION 4. To the fourth it must be said that, although there are many difficulties in the interpretation of Scripture, nevertheless, as Saint Augustine says: "If we are perplexed by an apparent contradiction in Scripture, it is not allowable to say that the author of this book is mistaken; but either the manuscript is faulty, or the translation is wrong, or you have not understood."[212] And if anyone should ask why God should have caused Scripture to contain so many obscurities and ambiguities, Augustine also says: "I do not doubt that all this was divinely arranged for the purpose of subduing pride by toil, and of preventing a feeling of satiety in the intellect, which generally holds in small esteem what is discovered without difficulty."[213]

REPLY TO OBJECTION 5. To the fifth it must be said that *Dei Verbum* §11 is ambiguous on this point, since the clause "for the sake of our salvation" could be understood not as limiting the scope of inerrancy but as giving the purpose of all Scripture, so that the sense would be that the books of sacred Scripture teach truth without any error, and that everything in them was put there by God for the sake of our salvation. Moreover, this latter interpretation fits better with what is said immediately before, namely: "Everything asserted by the inspired authors or sacred writers must be held to be asserted by the Holy Spirit."[214] For if the sacred writers erred in any of their assertions, and not only in those pertaining directly to human salvation, then the Holy Spirit would have erred, which is impossible. Moreover, the note on this

---

[212] Augustine, *Against Faustus* XI, 5.

[213] Augustine, *On Christian Doctrine* II, 6.

[214] Vatican II, *Dei Verbum*, §11.

text of *Dei Verbum* §11 references the teaching of *Providentissimus Deus* on the complete inerrancy of Scripture, which makes it absurd to suppose that it was simultaneously contradicting *Providentissimus Deus* on this point. However, even if *Dei Verbum* had contradicted the teaching of *Providentissimus Deus* in this matter, nothing would follow from this except that the Second Vatican Council would have taught error. For in cases of conflict between magisterial teaching, the less authoritative must give way to the more authoritative and the non-definitive to the definitive, as shown above (Q. 1, a. 2).

ARTICLE 11
Whether the Pope Speaks Infallibly in *Exsurge Domine*?

OBJECTION 1. It seems that the pope does not speak infallibly in *Exsurge Domine* (1520). For the propositions condemned therein are not condemned individually but only globally (*in globo*) as being "respectively heretical, or scandalous, or false, or offensive to pious ears, or seductive of simple minds, and against Catholic truth."[215] And according to Brian Harrison:

> A pope's condemnation of a proposition that may—for all he has told us—be no worse than "scandalous," "offensive to pious ears," or "seductive of simple minds," can certainly not qualify as an *ex cathedra* definition. For all those three lesser censures clearly involve the kind of judgment that might turn out to be reformable; whereas infallible definitions, of course, are by their very nature irreformable. (Assuming it is not certainly false, a given proposition that is nevertheless likely to "scandalize," "offend," or "seduce" the faithful

---

[215] Pope Leo X, *Exsurge Domine* (1520), §4.

under certain cultural/historical circumstances may not necessarily be so noxious under different circumstances.)[216]

OBJECTION 2. Furthermore, one of the propositions condemned in *Exsurge Domine* is this: "That heretics be burned is against the will of the Spirit."[217] But *Exsurge Domine* seems to err on this point, and so cannot be infallible. For anything that is intrinsically evil must be against the will of the Spirit. And capital punishment is intrinsically evil. For as it says in the revised text of the *Catechism of the Catholic Church*: "Consequently, the Church teaches, in the light of the Gospel, that 'the death penalty is inadmissible because it is an attack on the inviolability and dignity of the person.'"[218] And it can never be morally legitimate to attack the inviolability and dignity of the person.

OBJECTION 3. Furthermore, the burning of heretics constitutes a form of torture, which is also intrinsically evil. For the Second Vatican Council mentions torture, among other things, as an infamy that is a "supreme dishonor to the Creator."[219] Pope John Paul II cites the same list of things, including torture, as examples of intrinsically evil actions, saying: "They are such always and *per se*, in other words, on account of their very object, and quite apart from the ulterior intentions of the one acting and the circumstances."[220] And according to the *Catechism of the Catholic Church*: "*Torture* which uses physical or moral violence

---

[216] Brian W. Harrison, "Torture and Corporal Punishment as a Problem in Catholic Theology, Part II: The Witness of Tradition and Magisterium," *Living Tradition* 119 (Sep. 2005).

[217] Leo X, *Exsurge Domine*, condemned proposition 33.

[218] 2018 *Catechism of the Catholic Church* [henceforth: CCC], 2267.

[219] Vatican II, Pastoral Constitution on the Church in the Modern World, *Gaudium et Spes* (1965), §27.

[220] John Paul II, *Veritatis Splendor*, §80.

to extract confessions, punish the guilty, frighten opponents, or satisfy hatred is contrary to respect for the person and for human dignity."[221]

ON THE CONTRARY, according to Johann Baptist Franzelin, no Catholic can rightly deny that the propositions collectively condemned under diverse censures in *Exsurge Domine* are condemned infallibly.[222]

I ANSWER THAT, it must be said that Pope Leo X spoke *ex cathedra* when he condemned forty-one of the errors of Martin Luther in the following terms:

> With the advice and consent of these our venerable brothers, with mature deliberation on each and every one of the above theses, and by the authority of almighty God, the blessed Apostles Peter and Paul, and our own authority, we condemn, reprobate, and reject completely each of these theses or errors as respectively heretical, scandalous, false, offensive to pious ears or seductive of simple minds, and against Catholic truth. By listing them, we decree and declare that all the faithful of both sexes must regard them as condemned, reprobated, and rejected.[223]

The only doubt that arises with respect to the infallibility of this condemnation concerns the inclusion of several of the lesser censures, such as "scandalous" and "offensive to pious ears," within a global formula of condemnation, so that it is unclear which theological censure should be applied to which condemned proposition.

---

[221] 1997 CCC, 2297.

[222] Franzelin, *De divina traditione et scriptura*, 112–13.

[223] Leo X, *Exsurge Domine*, §4.

There are three schools of thought concerning this question. Some hold that such lesser censures do not involve a definite judgment of falsity, but merely proscribe a proposition as being somehow dangerous in the concrete circumstances of that time, while allowing for the possibility that they could be held and taught without danger at some future time.[224] Others hold that these censures do involve an infallible judgment of the falsity of the doctrine, since a true doctrine could not be so absolutely objectionable.[225] Still others hold that even though some of these censures do not involve a definite judgment of the falsity of the doctrine, there is still an infallible judgment as to the objectionable quality specified by the censure, so that the doctrine condemned as offensive to pious ears, for example, is permanently to be rejected and condemned as objectionable quality specified by the censure, so that the doctrine condemned as objectively offensive to pious ears, regardless of its inherent truth or falsity.[226]

This last position seems most in agreement with the mode of expression used by the pontiffs in condemnations of this kind. For the first position seems to minimize the definitive mode of the condemnation, while the second position seems to minimize the particular qualities of the censures employed.

However, this question need not be settled in order to accept the infallibility of the condemnations in *Exsurge Domine*. For in this instance it can be seen in other ways that Pope Leo X intended to exclude all the condemned propositions as objectively false and incompatible with the Catholic faith. In the first place, even though it is not clear which propositions are condemned as heretical, which as scandalous, which as offensive to pious ears,

---

[224] See, for example, Harrison, cited in the objection above.

[225] See, for example, Kleutgen, *Die Theologie*, 137.

[226] See, for example, Franzelin, *De divina traditione*, 113.

etc., nevertheless *all* of the propositions are condemned together as being "against Catholic truth" (*veritati catholicae obviantes*), for this last clause is introduced by the word "and" rather than "or."[227] Moreover, in the words immediately preceding the formula of condemnation, the pope gives the reason for this condemnation, saying:

> For according to these errors, or any one or several of them (*vel eorum aliquo vel aliquibus*), it clearly follows that the Church, which is guided by the Holy Spirit, is in error and has always erred. This is certainly against what Christ at his ascension promised to his disciples, as is read in the holy Gospel of Matthew: "I will be with you even to the consummation of the world." It is also against the determinations of the holy Fathers, and the express ordinances or canons of the Councils and the supreme Pontiffs.[228]

According to this explanation, which clearly manifests the mind and will of the pope, each and every individual error condemned in *Exsurge Domine* is to be rejected and condemned as being opposed at least by a logical consequence to a truth of divine revelation (namely, Mt 28:20), which places it squarely within the secondary object of infallibility. There can, therefore, be no remaining question as to whether the condemnations in *Exsurge Domine* are infallible.

OBJECTION 1. To the first it must be said that this objection overlooks the importance of the whole document in determining

---

[227] Leo X, *Exsurge Domine*, §4. For the Latin text, see Laerzio Cherubini, ed., *Magnum Bullarium Romanum* (Lyons: Borde and Arnaud, 1692–97), 1:615.

[228] Leo X, *Exsurge Domine*, §3.

the intended sense of the condemnation and ignores the crucial words "and against Catholic truth" (*et veritati catholicae obviantes*) within the formula of condemnation.

OBJECTION 2. To the second it must be said that capital punishment is not intrinsically evil. For according to the unanimous teaching of the Fathers of the Church,[229] from which no Catholic is permitted to depart,[230] God himself declares the moral right of the civil power to make use of the death penalty as just retribution for grave crimes, saying: "Whoever sheds the blood of man, by man shall his blood be shed; for God made man in his own image" (Gen 9:6); and again: "But if you do wrong, be afraid, for he [the civil ruler] does not bear the sword in vain; he is the servant of God to execute his wrath on the wrongdoer" (Rom 13:4). If, therefore, the revised text of the Catechism regarding capital punishment were to be understood as asserting that the death penalty is intrinsically evil, then it would have to be rejected as false and heretical. If, however, the revised text of the Catechism should be understood, as some have argued,[231] merely as a prudential judgment regarding the "admissibility" of using the death penalty in present contingent circumstances but

---

[229] For a review of the patristic sources, see Edward Feser and Joseph Bessette, *By Man Shall His Blood Be Shed: A Catholic Defense of Capital Punishment* (San Francisco: Ignatius Press, 2017); see also Avery Dulles, "Catholicism and Capital Punishment," *First Things* (April 2001).

[230] See: Council of Trent, *Decree on the Edition and Use of the Sacred Books* (1546); Vatican I, *Dei Filius*, ch. 2; Leo XIII, *Providentissimus Deus*, §14.

[231] See, for example: John Finnis, "Intentional Killing Is Always Wrong: The Development Initiated by Pius XII, Made by John Paul II, and Repeated by Francis," *Public Discourse*, August 22, 2018.

without denying its intrinsic legitimacy, then it would still have to be criticized as badly expressed (*male sonans*) and savoring of heresy (*sapiens haeresim*).

OBJECTION 3. To the third it must be said that the penalty of death by fire cannot be described as intrinsically evil without denying either the goodness of God or the divine inspiration of the Old Testament. For God himself in the law of Moses prescribes death by fire for certain crimes (cf. Lev 20:14; 21:9). In order to accept the teaching of Vatican II, Pope John Paul II, and the Catechism regarding the intrinsic evil of torture, therefore, we must say either that death by burning is not torture, which seems implausible; or that the meaning of the term "torture" is insufficiently clear, and this seems most likely. For "torture" may be used to mean the infliction of *severe* or *extreme* pain, and in this case it could not be described as intrinsically evil; or it could be used to mean the infliction of *excessive* pain, in which case it would be intrinsically evil by definition; or it could be used to refer to the kind of extra-judicial torture that prevails in modern times, that is, the *illegal* infliction of severe pain, which is intrinsically evil not on account of its severity as such but because it is "disproportionately cruel, or inflicted by unauthorized persons, or without due process, or inflicted on the innocent, or from sadistic motivations." According to Harrison, we should understand the modern condemnations of torture in this latter sense.[232]

ARTICLE 12
Whether the Pope Speaks Infallibly in *Unam Sanctam*?

OBJECTION 1. It seems that the pope does not speak infallibly in *Unam Sanctam* (1302). For that which is infallibly defined is

---

[232] Harrison, "Torture and Corporal Punishment."

irrevocable. But Pope Clement V revoked *Unam Sanctam* by his apostolic brief *Meruit* (1306).

OBJECTION 2. Furthermore, according to the Second Vatican Council: "The assent of the Church can never be wanting" to an infallible definition.[233] But most Catholics do not in fact assent to the teaching contained in *Unam Sanctam*. Therefore, it could not have been an infallible definition. As Sullivan says: "The eventual failure of any papal doctrine to be received by the Church as an article of its faith would show that the doctrine was not contained in the deposit of faith, and hence was not capable of being defined as dogma."[234]

ON THE CONTRARY, Billot and Dublanchy categorize *Unam Sanctam* as an *ex cathedra* definition.[235] Pope Pius XII also refers to the doctrine of this constitution as "the solemn teaching of Our predecessor of immortal memory Boniface VIII."[236]

I ANSWER THAT, it must be said that there could be no clearer instance of an *ex cathedra* definition than the declaration of Pope Boniface VIII at the conclusion of *Unam Sanctam*, where he says: "Furthermore, we declare, we proclaim, we define that it is absolutely necessary for salvation that every human creature be subject to the Roman Pontiff."[237] The only real question concerns the rest of the document—whether any more of its teaching is infallible or only the final definition. In response to this it must be said that there are in fact many infallible doctrinal assertions in this document. For the opening lines of the constitution are explicitly

---

[233] Vatican II, *Lumen Gentium*, §25.
[234] Sullivan, *Creative Fidelity*, 88.
[235] Billot, *Tractatus de Ecclesia Christi*, 642; Dublanchy, "Infaillibilité," 1703.
[236] Pope Pius XII, Encyclical Letter *Mystici Corporis* (1943), §40.
[237] Pope Boniface VIII, Bull *Unam Sanctam* (1302).

definitive, saying: "Urged by faith, *we are obliged to believe* and to maintain that the Church is one, holy, catholic, and also apostolic. *We believe in her firmly* and we confess with simplicity that outside of her there is neither salvation nor the remission of sins."[238]

The doctrinal content of the main body of the constitution is then presented largely without such explicitly definitive language, and yet it is one of these assertions which Pius XII identifies as the "solemn teaching" of Boniface VIII, saying: "That Christ and his Vicar constitute one only head is the solemn teaching of Our predecessor of immortal memory Boniface VIII in the apostolic letter *Unam Sanctam*."[239]

Finally, there is more explicitly definitive language toward the close of the constitution where it says: "*With truth as our witness*, it belongs to spiritual power to establish the terrestrial power and to pass judgement if it has not been good." And again: "Therefore whoever resists this power thus ordained by God, resists the ordinance of God (Rom 13:2), unless he invent like Manicheus two beginnings, *which is false and judged by us heretical*."[240]

REPLY TO OBJECTION 1. To the first it must be said that Pope Clement V did not actually revoke or contradict in any way the solemn teaching of *Unam Sanctam*. In order to appease King Philip IV of France, he merely explained that *Unam Sanctam* had not made temporal rulers subject to the authority of the Church in any way other than they had been formerly, saying:

> Therefore, we will and intend that no prejudice be engendered against the king and kingdom by the definition and declaration of our predecessor Boniface VIII, of happy

[238] Boniface VIII, *Unam Sanctam*.
[239] Pius XII, *Mystici Corporis*, §40.
[240] Boniface VIII, *Unam Sanctam*.

memory, which begins *Unam Sanctam*; and that neither the king, kingdom, nor the inhabitants thereof be more subjected to the Church of Rome than they were before; but that all things be understood as remaining in the same state in which they were before the aforesaid definition, both as regards the Church and as regards the aforesaid king, kingdom, and inhabitants thereof.[241]

REPLY TO OBJECTION 2. To the second it must be said that to make the authority of a solemn papal definition dependent upon its reception by the Church is a complete inversion of the proper relationship between authority and faith. Lack of reception of this teaching or of any other dogma of the Church, even by a great number of Catholics, is evidence only of their ignorance or heresy, and not of the genuine *sensus fidelium*.

---

[241] Pope Clement V, *Meruit* (1306).

Part II

Essays on Papal Authority

1

On the Modes of Exercise
of the Magisterium

The State of the Question

If one consults books, internet articles, etc., on the various modes
of operation of the Church's magisterium, one is likely to find
a bewildering array of differing descriptions of the matter with
different theologians using the terms "extraordinary magisterium,"
"ordinary magisterium," and "ordinary and universal magisterium"
in different ways to mean different things.

Most theologians agree that the "extraordinary magisterium"
refers to the solemn and infallible judgments or definitions of
popes and ecumenical councils. But they disagree about what
counts as a solemn judgment or definition.

1. Some would include any proposition of a matter of
   faith or morals that is set forth *in a definitive way*, that
   is, with the manifest intention of obliging the faithful
   to hold or believe it.
2. Others would include only the definitive proposition
   of *dogmas*, that is, matters of faith or morals set forth
   specifically as divinely revealed truths.
3. Still others would restrict this category still further to
   include only the definitive proposition of *new dogmas*,
   that is, matters of faith or morals set forth as divinely

revealed truths which up until then had been open to legitimate dispute.[242]

Then regarding the "ordinary and universal magisterium," most theologians agree that this is exercised by the college of bishops in union with the pope in their state of dispersion throughout the world.

1. Some, taking the term "universal" to refer to this universal dispersion of the bishops, extend their use of the term "ordinary and universal magisterium" no further than this.

2. But others, taking the term "universal" to refer instead to the universality of the episcopal college itself, also apply the term "ordinary and universal magisterium" to the non-solemn teaching of ecumenical councils.

3. Still others, taking the term "universal" to refer to the extension of authority over the universal Church, also apply the term "ordinary and universal magisterium" to the magisterium of the pope when he is teaching the universal Church without speaking *ex cathedra*.

I will argue in this essay that the first position is the correct one.

Finally, there is the term "ordinary magisterium" without the addition of "universal." Most theologians agree that this category includes whatever is left over from the other two categories, though the details of what exactly is included here will vary greatly depending on how broadly or restrictively one understands those other two categories.

The Question of Infallibility

As if all this weren't enough, there is also the question of infallibility. Most theologians agree that the extraordinary magisterium is

---

[242] I argue that the first position is the correct one in q. 1, aa. 4–5, above.

always infallible and that the ordinary and universal magisterium at least can be infallible (some hold that it is always infallible). And most agree that the ordinary magisterium (non-universal) is not infallible.

The most significant diversity of opinion turns on how one deals with the fact that the Church teaches (e.g., in *Lumen Gentium* 25): that the pope and ecumenical councils are infallible when they *define* doctrine (extraordinary magisterium); and that the bishops dispersed throughout the world are infallible when they propose a doctrine as *definitively to be held* (ordinary and universal magisterium). Why do the bishops appear to have two modes of infallible teaching while the pope has only one?

1.) Most theologians hold that the proposition of a doctrine as *definitively to be held* by a pope or a council is not enough to constitute a *definition* of the extraordinary magisterium.

    a.) Some of these, arguing that the pope's infallibility cannot be more limited than the bishops' and that the bishops gathered in council cannot have less authority than the same bishops dispersed throughout the world, conclude that when a pope or a council proposes a doctrine as *definitively to be held*, they do so infallibly in virtue of the ordinary and universal magisterium.

    b.) Others argue that the "dissymmetry" in the Church's teaching between papal and episcopal infallibility is deliberate and that there is no such thing as an infallible ordinary magisterium of the pope or an infallible papal exercise of the ordinary and universal magisterium, so that a pope who proposes a doctrine as *definitively to be held* does not do so infallibly whereas the bishops dispersed throughout the world (and perhaps also the bishops gathered in council?) are infallible when they propose a doctrine as definitively to be held.

    c.) Another option, however, which is mostly overlooked on account of the confusion about the nature of the extraordinary magisterium, is to deny the presupposition of both the above positions and hold instead that the proposition of a doctrine as *definitively to be held* by a pope or an ecumenical council simply is a *definition* and that the bishops' unique mode of *teaching definitively without defining* is due to the state of dispersion in which it occurs. (I hold that this last position is the correct one.)

A Question of Context

I am convinced that the root of the confusion surrounding these issues is the assumption that the terminology of ordinary and extraordinary magisterium refers to just one distinction, whereas in fact it applies to two separate but overlapping distinctions in two separate but overlapping contexts. The result is that the term "ordinary magisterium" in particular is highly ambiguous (it means different things in different contexts) and thus arguments involving the term "ordinary magisterium" easily fall into the fallacy of equivocation.

    Let me begin by setting out these two different contexts in which the terminology of ordinary and extraordinary arises. The original context is that of the rule of faith (*regula fidei*) within the field of fundamental theology. The focus here is on the nature of divine revelation, the virtue of faith as man's response to divine revelation, the relationship between faith and reason, Scripture and Tradition as the sources of divine revelation, and the role of the Church in safeguarding and transmitting divine revelation. At

Vatican I, this was treated in *Dei Filius*, the dogmatic constitution on the Catholic faith; at Vatican II, this was treated in *Dei Verbum*, the dogmatic constitution on divine revelation.

The second context in which the same terminology arises is the nature of the Church within the field of ecclesiology. The focus here is on the nature of the Church, the members of the Church, the hierarchical structure of the Church, authority and jurisdiction in the Church, the Church's mission of teaching, governing, and sanctifying, etc. At Vatican I, this was treated in *Pastor Aeternus*, the first dogmatic constitution on the Church of Christ (a second constitution was intended but never completed); at Vatican II, this was treated in *Lumen Gentium*, the dogmatic constitution on the Church.

The Origins of the Terminology

The terminology of ordinary and extraordinary magisterium seems to have originated in the nineteenth century and entered the mainstream of theological vocabulary especially through the influence of the German Jesuit neo-scholastic theologian Joseph Kleutgen in the context of his treatise on the rule of faith. The first question he set out to answer in his massive and highly influential work *Die Theologie der Vorzeit verteidigt* (a defense of scholastic theology) was this: What are Catholics obliged to believe? And his principal concern in answering this question was to oppose the dogmatic minimalism, especially prevalent in contemporary German theology, according to which Catholics are obliged to believe only what has been formally and infallibly defined by the Church. Against this idea, he asserts that the Church exercises a double magisterium: the one is "ordinary and perpetual" (*ordentlich und immerwährend*) and it consists in all those ongoing apostolates of the Church by which the faith is handed down through the living tradition; the other is "extraordinary" (*außerordentlich*) and is used only at special times when false teachers disturb the Church.[243]

What did he mean by these terms and what exactly was the nature of the distinction between them? In Kleutgen's works, the term "extraordinary magisterium" refers to the explicit definitions of the Church in matters of faith and morals.[244] Let us look at each part of this definition in turn:

- The object of the extraordinary magisterium is "matters of faith and morals," whether contained directly in the deposit of faith (primary object) or intrinsically connected to the deposit of faith (secondary object).

- The subject of the extraordinary magisterium is "the Church," which means that it can be exercised only by those who bear supreme authority in the Church, namely the pope and the college of bishops (which includes the pope).

- The act of the extraordinary magisterium is the act of "definition," which means that the doctrine in question is proposed to the Church in a definitive or conclusive way as something that must be *firmly believed* or *definitively held*.

- The distinguishing feature of the extraordinary magisterium as compared with the ordinary magisterium lies in the fact that its definitive teaching is "explicit," which means that it is visibly and tangibly enshrined in a public document of the magisterium.

---

[243] Joseph Kleutgen, *Die Theologie der Vorzeit vertheidigt*, vol. 1, 1st ed. (Münster: Theissing, 1853), 47.

[244] See especially Kleutgen, *Die Theologie*, 40–46.

What, then, does Kleutgen intend by the term "ordinary magisterium"? This term refers to the organic transmission of the contents of divine revelation through the living tradition of the Church.[245] Let us again look at each part of this definition:

- The object of the ordinary magisterium is "the contents of divine revelation," which is the same as saying "matters of faith and morals."
- The subject of the ordinary magisterium is again "the Church," which Kleutgen specifies as meaning the body of bishops in union with their head the pope.[246]
- The activity of the ordinary magisterium is the "organic transmission" of divine revelation, which refers to the daily teaching, preaching, and handing on of the faith that occurs within the Church through her "living tradition."
- The distinguishing feature of the ordinary magisterium as compared with the extraordinary magisterium lies in its relative intangibility; it is the infallible teaching of the Church that occurs *apart from* the formal and visible documents of the Church's magisterium.

The last point requires further explanation. The teaching of the extraordinary magisterium is found by looking within the documents of the magisterium; the teaching of the ordinary magisterium, by contrast, is found by looking *outside* the formal teaching documents of the magisterium to *all the other sources of the living tradition*, and in the first place to Scripture itself. Since the Church proposes all of Scripture as the divinely revealed word of God, as soon as one sees that a truth is clearly proposed in Scripture,

---

[245] See especially Kleutgen, *Die Theologie*, 46–53.
[246] Kleutgen, *Die Theologie*, 42.

one can also see that it is proposed by the Church as a divinely revealed truth and so one must accept and believe it as a dogma of faith (infallibly taught by the ordinary magisterium). It would be heresy to deny, for example, that Christ was transfigured on the mount, that the Holy Family fled to Egypt, or that Christians have a moral duty to love their enemies, even though none of these things has been formally defined by the Church. And then together with Sacred Scripture one looks to the writings of the Church Fathers, who are the privileged witnesses of Sacred Tradition, and then also to the Doctors of the Church and other eminent Catholic theologians, to the customs, liturgies, and laws of the Church, to the monuments of antiquity, the consensus of the faithful, and finally, the statements of individual bishops and local councils.

Kleutgen's main purpose in speaking at all about an "ordinary magisterium" was to re-assert against the dogmatic minimalists of his time (who are still with us today) the binding authority of the living tradition of the Church; he wanted to re-direct our attention away from an obsessive fixation on the formal teaching documents of the Church toward the broader horizons and greater depths of the entire living tradition. At the same time, however, he was wary of asserting the authority of Scripture and Tradition apart from the explicit judgments of the Church without linking them in some way to the magisterium in order to maintain (against the Protestant principle of private interpretation) the Catholic principle of ecclesiastical mediation according to which Catholics believe all that and only that which God has revealed and which has been proposed as such by the Church. Hence his reinterpretation of the living tradition of the Church, by which Scripture and the oral Tradition are perpetually handed down in the Church, as an exercise of the magisterium of the Church.

There are two concluding points worth emphasizing about Kleutgen's understanding of the ordinary magisterium.

First, the ordinary magisterium is exercised only by the whole Church in its state of being dispersed throughout the world for the quite simple and obvious reason that the teaching of popes and ecumenical councils is necessarily found in or given by formal and explicit acts of teaching formulated in public documents of the supreme magisterium (which is exactly what the teaching of the ordinary magisterium is not). Hence, for Kleutgen it would be quite absurd to talk about an ecumenical council or a pope exercising the ordinary magisterium.

Second, in Kleutgen's writings there is no distinction between an "ordinary magisterium" and an "ordinary and universal magisterium." There is only one ordinary magisterium, which is universal by nature and always infallible. Because he is writing in the context of the rule of faith, only the infallible teaching of the Church comes into view, for only infallible teaching can oblige the faithful to give an assent of faith. Non-infallible teaching does not constitute part of the rule of faith because the response due to the non-infallible but still authoritative teaching of the Church is a religious submission (*obsequium religiosum*) but not the submission of faith (*obsequium fidei*). The distinction between the ordinary and the extraordinary magisterium occurs for Kleutgen within the context of the Church's infallible teaching as a distinction between doctrines that have been defined as of faith (*de fide definita*) and doctrines that are of faith even without having been defined as such (*de fide non definita*).

Pope Pius IX and Vatican I

The substance of Kleutgen's teaching on the ordinary magisterium was taken up and confirmed by Pope Pius IX in the apostolic letter *Tuas Libenter* and by the First Vatican Council in the dogmatic constitution *Dei Filius*. In each of these documents the same distinction (between the explicit judgments or definitions of the Church and the ordinary magisterium of the Church) is introduced in the same context (the rule of faith) in order to oppose the same problem (dogmatic minimalism). Here is how Pope Pius IX puts it:

> For even if it were a matter of that submission which must be manifested by an act of divine faith, nevertheless, this would not have to be limited to those matters that have been *defined by explicit decrees* of ecumenical councils or by the Roman pontiffs and by this Apostolic See, but would also have to be extended to those matters *transmitted* as divinely revealed *by the ordinary magisterium of the whole Church dispersed throughout the world* and, for that reason, held by the universal and constant consensus of Catholic theologians as belonging to the faith.[247]

In the words of Vatican I:

> All those things are to be believed with divine and Catholic faith that are contained in the word of God, written or handed down, and which by the Church, *either in solemn judgment or through her ordinary and universal magisterium*, are proposed for belief as having been divinely revealed.[248]

The discussions that took place among the fathers of the First Vatican Council and the official explanations and clarifications of the intended meaning of the text that can be found in the conciliar

[247] *Tuas Libenter*, Denz. 2879.
[248] *Dei Filius*, Denz. 3011.

acta make it clear that the intended sense of this distinction in the conciliar text corresponds closely to the way in which Kleutgen understood it. An important point is that the word "universal" was added to the term "ordinary magisterium" specifically in order to express the same thing that Pius IX had expressed in speaking of the "ordinary magisterium dispersed throughout the world" and in order to make it clear that the text did not speak about a papal exercise of the magisterium.[249]

At this juncture there is no distinction between an "ordinary magisterium" and an "ordinary and universal magisterium." The ordinary magisterium simply is universal in the sense that it is exercised by the Church dispersed throughout the world (as opposed to by the pope or an ecumenical council). No explanation of this is given in the magisterial texts themselves, but if we understand that the ordinary magisterium refers to the transmission of Scripture and Tradition through the living tradition outside the documents of the magisterium, then it makes perfect sense why this must be the case.

A Shift in Meaning and Application

Following the First Vatican Council, however, an important shift occurred in the understanding and use of these terms. After the definition of papal infallibility, it was generally understood that the pope exercised the extraordinary magisterium in his solemn definitions *ex cathedra*; but many of the magisterial acts of the popes clearly fell short of being *ex cathedra definitions*; thus they were attributed to an ordinary magisterium exercised by the pope. The concept of an "ordinary papal magisterium" was thus born, and this had several effects.

[249] Mansi 51:322.

The first effect was a distortion in the original meaning of the term "ordinary magisterium." Since this "ordinary" teaching of the popes (for example, in their encyclical letters) was quite explicit and documented, Kleutgen's emphasis on the ordinary magisterium as a means of transmitting the faith *apart from* the explicit documents of the hierarchy faded from view. The concept of an ordinary magisterium, which had been intended to move beyond a narrow focus on the statements of the hierarchy toward a broader view of the rule of faith grounded in Scripture, Tradition, the liturgy, etc., was reinterpreted as just another kind of magisterial document.

A further result of this distortion was a new application of the same terminology of ordinary and extraordinary magisterium to a different distinction. The same terminology that had been used within the context of the rule of faith to distinguish between *defined* and *undefined* doctrines of faith, now began to be applied within the context of the evaluation of individual acts of magisterial teaching to distinguish between *definitive* and *non-definitive* acts of explicitly documented magisterial teaching. And this new distinction has been superimposed upon the original distinction, as illustrated on the facing page:

Original 19th Century Conception (Context of the Rule of Faith)

	(Infallible)
Explicitly Documented	Extraordinary Magisterium
Not Explicitly Documented	Ordinary Magisterium

20th Century Development (Context of the Acts of Magisterial Teaching)

	Infallible	Non-Infallible
(Explicitly Documented)	Extraordinary Magisterium	Ordinary Magisterium

Combined View (Overlapping Contexts)

	Infallible	Non-Infallible
Explicitly Documented	Extraordinary Magisterium	Ordinary (Authentic) Magisterium
Not Explicitly Documented	Ordinary (Universal) Magisterium	

The root of the difficulty is this: if the extraordinary magisterium is the organ of Church teaching that is at once both *explicit* and *definitive*, then two very different kinds of teaching can be contrasted against it, and both will appear to be "ordinary" by comparison. One is the teaching of the Church that is *definitive* but *not explicit*, and this is what Kleutgen had in mind, and what was intended by the term "ordinary magisterium" as it was used by Pius IX and by Vatican I. The other is the teaching of the Church that is *explicit* but *not definitive*, and this appears to be what Pius XII, for example, has in mind in *Humani generis* when he calls for a religious assent (but not an assent of faith) to the teaching contained in papal encyclical letters. The former "ordinary magisterium" is the infallible living tradition itself; the latter "ordinary magisterium" is the authentic but not infallible magisterium of the pope and bishops. These are completely opposite forms of teaching, sharing in common only the fact that neither is a third thing, namely the extraordinary magisterium. Calling them both by the same name is a little bit like calling angels and apes by the same name simply because neither are men.

Let me repeat that point. I am convinced that the most important thing to understand, in order to get clarity regarding the ordinary and extraordinary magisterium, is that this terminology covers not one distinction but two. One usage refers to the distinction between *defined* and *undefined* doctrines taught infallibly by the Church; another usage refers to the distinction between *infallible* and *merely authentic* acts of teaching. And whereas the meaning of the term "extraordinary" is the same in both cases, the two meanings of "ordinary" are very different. It is this ambiguity of the term "ordinary magisterium" that breeds constant confusion and derails so many arguments having to do with the magisterium.

Vatican II

The Second Vatican Council completely avoided the use of the terminology of ordinary and extraordinary magisterium in its constitution on the Church *Lumen Gentium*, which outlines three basic forms of magisterial teaching: (1) the authentic (i.e., authoritative) but not infallible teaching of the pope and bishops; (2) the infallible definitions of popes and ecumenical councils; and (3) the infallible teaching of the bishops dispersed throughout the world (a footnote referring to *Tuas Libenter* and *Dei Filius* makes it clear that this is a reference to the ordinary and universal magisterium).

I believe that much confusion could be avoided if we were to follow the example of *Lumen Gentium* in speaking consistently of the "authentic magisterium" of popes and bishops when it is a question of their non-infallible teaching, while reserving the term "ordinary magisterium" for the infallible teaching of the Church dispersed throughout the world.

And we would do well to pay closer attention to employing the right distinction in the right context. When it is a question of evaluating the degree of authority exercised in an individual act of teaching and the response owed to that particular act of teaching, the relevant distinction is between definitive and non-definitive acts of teaching; that is, between the exercise of the infallible magisterium or the merely authentic magisterium (following the terminology of *Lumen Gentium*, where the context is the magisterium).

When it is a question of evaluating the status of a given doctrine and the source of our obligation to believe or hold that doctrine, then the relevant distinction is between defined and undefined doctrines taught by the Church; that is, between the solemn judgments (extraordinary magisterium) and the ordinary magisterium (following the terminology of *Dei Filius*, where the context is the rule of faith).

The ambiguity of the term "ordinary magisterium" makes this topic unnecessarily complex. If we would only resolve the ambiguity by substituting the term "authentic magisterium" for "ordinary magisterium" whenever we are dealing with magisterial documents that do not contain solemn definitions, the whole question would immediately become much clearer and simpler, which would be a good thing if our goal is clarity and truth rather than confusion and obfuscation.

In the first part of this essay, I attempted to cut through some of the confusion that frequently surrounds discussions of the various modes of exercise of the magisterium, particularly with reference to the term "ordinary magisterium," which can mean two different things in two different contexts.

To recap briefly, the original meaning of the term "ordinary magisterium," as it was intended to be understood when it was introduced into theological vocabulary in the nineteenth century, referred to the infallible transmission of divine revelation (Scripture and Tradition) through the living tradition of the Church *apart from* the official documents of the supreme magisterium (popes and ecumenical councils). Over the course of time, the same term came to be used to refer to the teaching *contained in* the magisterial documents of popes and ecumenical councils whenever this teaching fell short of being an extraordinary definition. The first ordinary magisterium (often called the "ordinary and universal magisterium") is infallible; the second ordinary magisterium (sometimes called the "authentic magisterium") is not infallible.

How to Evaluate Magisterial Documents

When evaluating the degree of authority of the teaching contained in any individual papal document (or ecumenical council *mutatis mutandis*), the first step is to identify what judgments are being proposed in matters of faith or morals (as opposed to purely disciplinary legislation or assertions about other areas of human knowledge not connected with faith or morals). The next step is to identify the *quality* or *note* of the doctrinal proposition:

1. If a doctrine is proposed as one that *must be firmly believed as divinely revealed*, then we have an infallible definition of dogma by the extraordinary magisterium of the pope speaking *ex cathedra*. The response due to this kind of teaching is the assent of divine faith. Its rejection would be heresy.

2. If a doctrine is proposed as one that *must be definitively held as certainly true*, then we have an infallible definition of doctrine by the extraordinary magisterium of the pope speaking *ex cathedra*. The response due to this kind of teaching is a firm and definitive assent based on faith in the Church's infallibility in these matters. To reject such a doctrine would separate one from full communion with the Church.

3. If a doctrine is proposed as *true* but without the note of definitive obligation or absolute certainty, then we have an authoritative (but not infallible) proposition of doctrine by the authentic magisterium of the pope. The response due to this kind of teaching is a religious submission of will and intellect. Failure to assent to this kind of teaching, without grave reason, would be rash.

4. If a doctrine is proposed merely as *possible* or *probable*, then it does not rise to the level of magisterial teaching and does not impose any obligation of assent or adherence.

The Case of *Amoris Laetitia*

In the case of *Amoris Laetitia*, there is a general consensus that it represents, at least in the main, an exercise of the authentic magisterium (category 3 above), though there may be portions of the text that don't even rise to that level.

The kind of response owed to this kind of teaching is specified by Vatican II in *Lumen Gentium* 25 where it says that a "religious submission of mind and will must be shown in a special way to the authentic magisterium of the Roman Pontiff, even when he is not speaking *ex cathedra*." There is a lengthy discussion in the 1990 CDF document *Donum Veritatis* (§§ 23–31) about what this kind of response entails. To put the matter briefly, a genuine internal assent to the truth of the teaching is generally expected, although there can be cases where it is legitimate to withhold this kind of assent for serious reasons. This is because we are dealing precisely with the *non-infallible* teaching of the Church, which by definition *could be mistaken*; at the same time, since the Church enjoys a special divine assistance in the exercise of her mission, even when the charism of infallibility is not involved, it would be wrong to conclude that the Church could be *habitually mistaken* at this level.

A Particularly Egregious Exaggeration of Authority

Stephen Walford, in his February 2, 2017 piece in the *Vatican Insider*, takes this "charism of special assistance" as his point of departure for constructing an argument on the basis of which he concludes: "We must affirm that Pope Francis *cannot possibly be in error* in his ordinary magisterium concerning issues of faith and morals, and thus his teaching that under certain, carefully considered cases, Holy Communion can be given to persons in irregular situations is perfectly valid and influenced by the Holy Spirit."[250]

That is an audacious claim. Let's try to follow the steps of his argument. His first premise, drawn from Pope John Paul II's commentary on *Lumen Gentium* 25 in his Wednesday Audience of March 17, 1993, is that the ordinary magisterium of the pope enjoys a "charism of special assistance" even when he is not speaking *ex cathedra*. So far, so good. He then adds that *Amoris Laetitia* is an exercise of the ordinary magisterium, which is unobjectionable as long as we understand that the term "ordinary magisterium" in this context refers to the "authentic magisterium" of the pope not speaking *ex cathedra* and not to the "ordinary magisterium" of the Church throughout the world, which is infallible. These are, as I argued above, two very different things.

Walford continues: "Can a Pope teach error in his ordinary magisterium in matters of faith and morals? St John Paul's answer is a definite no."

Now to say that the pope "cannot teach error" in his ordinary magisterium is the same as saying that the pope is infallible in his ordinary magisterium. That's just what infallible means: "unable to fail" in its purpose, which is teaching truth. Prior to Vatican II it was fairly common for theologians to argue that the ordinary magisterium of the pope is infallible, but this is a rare claim these days. Does John Paul II really teach this? Walford quotes a text that does seem to support the idea: "Alongside this infallibility of

---

[250] Emphasis mine.

ex cathedra definitions, there is the charism of the Holy Spirit's assistance, granted to Peter and his successors so that they would not err in matters of faith and morals, but rather shed great light on the Christian people. This charism is not limited to exceptional cases."[251]

I have to admit that the first time I read this text I also thought that John Paul II was endorsing the infallibility of the ordinary papal magisterium. But one of my theology professors at the time helpfully drew my attention to some other remarks that John Paul II makes in the same context. In his Audience of March 10, 1993, he contrasts the ordinary papal magisterium with the *ex cathedra* definitions of the pope, which he identifies with the extraordinary magisterium; then in the Audience of March 24, 1993, he clearly asserts that the pope speaks infallibly only (*"solo"* in the original Italian) when he speaks *ex cathedra*. Taken together these statements exclude an infallible exercise of the ordinary papal magisterium. So if we are to assume that John Paul II is not just contradicting himself, we have to interpret the statement quoted by Walford as referring to a *general* protection from *habitual error* rather than an *infallible* protection from *all error*.

Walford's next authority is Pope Innocent III, who says: "The Lord clearly intimates that Peter's successors will never at any time deviate from the Catholic faith, but will instead recall the others and strengthen the hesitant."[252]

What Walford needed to do at this point was to show that these words apply not only to the *ex cathedra* definitions of the popes but also to their teaching when they are not speaking *ex cathedra*. Instead he turns aside to the question about whether a pope can

---

[251] John Paul II, Wednesday Audience of March 24, 1993.
[252] Pope Innocent III, *Apostolicae Sedis Primatus*, 1199.

fall into heresy as a "private theologian," which is really irrelevant to the question of *Amoris Laetitia* unless Cardinal Burke is right that it does not even rise to the level of being an act of the magisterium. In any case, however, the idea that the pope cannot fall into error as a private theologian has never been more than the private opinion of some theologians; it has never been endorsed by the Church.

Next up is a pair of even less relevant quotes from Pope Pius XII, which demonstrate the "supreme importance of the papacy." Since when was that the point at issue?

Then there is some meandering commentary about how the popes have the task of teaching the truth, supporting the truth, and guarding the true faith not only in their *ex cathedra* definitions but also in their ordinary teaching, which is all absolutely true and does absolutely nothing to prove that they receive the additional grace to do all of this *infallibly* in their ordinary (authentic) magisterium.

Finally, Walford appeals to the text of Pope Pius IX's *Tuas Libenter*, in which we are reminded that the dogmatic teaching of the Church is not limited to the solemn definitions of popes and ecumenical councils but includes the dogmatic teaching of the ordinary magisterium of the Church dispersed throughout the world. Walford offers no commentary on this text but simply moves directly to his conclusion that "Pope Francis cannot possibly be in error in his ordinary magisterium concerning issues of faith and morals," and thus to "his teaching that under certain, carefully considered cases, Holy Communion can be given to persons in irregular situations."

This, however, completely overlooks the fact that Pius IX was speaking explicitly about the authority of the ordinary magisterium *of the Church dispersed throughout the world*, which is, as I argued earlier, an allusion to the *living tradition of the whole Church*, and not to the magisterial teaching of the popes when they are not speaking *ex cathedra*.

I have to admit that it can seem very tempting to reason that the ordinary magisterium of the pope must be infallible because the ordinary magisterium of the bishops dispersed throughout the world is infallible. But to do so is to commit the fallacy of equivocation, because the term "ordinary magisterium" means different things when applied to the Church dispersed throughout the world and when applied to the pope. In the former case, it means the *infallible* teaching of the living tradition transmitted *apart from* the documents of the magisterium; in the latter case, it means the *non-infallible* teaching of the pope and bishops *contained in* the documents of the magisterium. Once the terms are clearly understood the argument contains its own refutation.

Before ending, Walford throws off a couple of rhetorical questions and cites some additional authorities to reinforce his position. He asks: "Do we then pick and choose which teachings of which popes to accept? That would be tantamount to a form of Protestantism. The Council of Lyons stated the Pope 'has the duty to defend the truth of the faith, and it is his responsibility to resolve all disputed matters in the area of faith.'"

I answer: We accept all of the infallible teachings of all of the popes and we accept all of the non-infallible teachings of all of the popes insofar as they do not conflict with the infallible teaching of the Church. I fail to see anything very Protestant about that. And the citation of Lyons is, of course, true—but once again beside the point. Popes defend the truth and resolve disputed questions of faith above all through their *ex cathedra* definitions. Indeed, that is the principal purpose of *ex cathedra* definitions. If Walford wants to argue that this text of Lyons goes beyond *ex cathedra* definitions, he will have to provide some reasons for thinking so.

Then he asks: "If protection from the Lord were only to apply to rare *ex cathedra* declarations how could all disputes of faith possibly be resolved? We must remember St Ambrose's famous phrase: 'Where Peter is, there is the Church. Where the Church is, there is no death but life eternal.'"

I answer: All disputes of faith could be resolved by *ex cathedra* definitions, which need not be as rare as they are and probably are much less rare than Walford supposes. They are rare only by comparison with the ordinary (universal) magisterium, which is exercised every day in the preaching and teaching by which the faith is handed down all over the world. Even several *ex cathedra* definitions per month would still be rare by comparison. At the First Vatican Council, in the official explanation of the intended sense of the definition of papal infallibility, Bishop Vincent Gasser, speaking on behalf of the deputation charged with the drafting of the definition, remarked that it was impossible to specify the form in which *ex cathedra* definitions had to be given, since "already thousands and thousands of dogmatic judgments have gone forth from the Apostolic See."[253] Granted, this is not part of the definition itself, but the understanding of the text as presented in Gasser's speech was the basis upon which the council fathers voted to pass and promulgate the text, so it counts for something in determining the right interpretation of the text of Vatican I.

As for St. Ambrose's famous phrase: "Where Peter is, there is the Church. Where the Church is, there is no death but life eternal," this is a beautiful expression of the necessity for salvation

[253] Mansi 52:1215.

of membership in the Roman Catholic Church and of the primacy of Rome as the center of the Church's unity. But I thought we were arguing about whether the ordinary papal magisterium is infallible?

To paraphrase Walford's concluding lines, I would say that if we claim to hold Tradition dear, if we claim to defend Tradition with all our strength, then we must accept and defend the magisterium of Pope Francis insofar as it does not deviate from Tradition. There is no other interpretation available; the Church has spoken.

Donum Veritatis on Non-Infallible Church Teaching

Since *Amoris Laetitia* does not contain any *ex cathedra* definitions, and since the pope is infallible only when he defines *ex cathedra*, the charism of infallibility is not involved in *Amoris Laetitia*. But since *Amoris Laetitia* does contain teaching in matters of faith and morals, and since the authentic magisterium of the pope is engaged in such teaching even when it is not *ex cathedra*, the charism of divine assistance is potentially involved in *Amoris Laetitia*, and this charism excludes the probability but not the possibility of error.

What to do if it does contain error? The CDF, in the instruction *Donum Veritatis*, 24, says this: "It can happen, however, that a theologian may, according to the case, raise questions regarding the timeliness, the form, or even the contents of magisterial interventions." A theologian who finds himself unable to assent to some teaching of the authentic papal magisterium should not present his own opinions as though they were non-arguable conclusions (DV 27). And he should "refrain from giving *untimely* public expression to them" (DV 27), which implies that there may be a timely public expression of disagreement. And then, DV 30:

If, despite a loyal effort on the theologian's part, the difficulties persist, the theologian has the duty to make known to the Magisterial authorities the problems raised by the teaching in itself, in the arguments proposed to justify it, or even in the manner in which it is presented. He should do this in an evangelical spirit and with a profound desire to resolve the difficulties. His objections could then contribute to real progress and provide a stimulus to the Magisterium to propose the teaching of the Church in greater depth and with a clearer presentation of the arguments.

In the case of *Amoris Laetitia*, it seems clear to me that this is exactly the course of action that the Cardinals who submitted the *dubia* to Pope Francis were faithfully trying to pursue—nor should we fail to take into account the *Code of Canon Law*, 212, 3:

> According to the knowledge, competence, and prestige which they possess, they [viz., the Christian faithful] have have the right and even at times the duty to manifest to the sacred pastors their opinion on matters which pertain to the good of the Church and to make their opinion known to the rest of the Christian faithful, without prejudice to the integrity of faith and morals, with reverence toward their pastors, and attentive to common advantage and the dignity of persons.

2

Authentic Magisterium and Religious Submission

In the discussions prompted by the publication in the *Acta Apostolicae Sedis* (AAS) of two documents pertaining to the interpretation of *Amoris Laetitia*, many people seem to have picked up the idea that the authentic magisterium is infallible, as if this were a case of *Roma locuta, causa finita est*. But this is not true. Whatever else this recent publication in the AAS may mean, it does not mean that anything has been definitively answered or decided.

The authentic magisterium, to which the faithful owe religious submission of will and intellect (*Lumen Gentium* 25; cf. CIC 752), is not infallible.[254] This is what *Lumen Gentium* says about the authentic magisterium of the pope and the bishops:

> In matters of faith and morals, the bishops speak in the name of Christ, and the faithful are to accept their teaching and adhere to it with a religious submission of the soul

[254] The term "authentic magisterium" can be used in a broad or a narrow sense: in a broad sense, it can be used to refer to all official magisterial teaching, whether infallible or not; it is usually used in a more narrow sense to refer to official teaching that is not infallible, but is still authoritative. This is the sense in which it is being used here.

(*religioso animi obsequio*). This religious submission of will
and intellect (*religiosum voluntatis et intellectus obsequium*)
must be shown in a special way to the authentic Magisterium of the Roman pontiff, even when he is not speaking
ex cathedra; that is, it must be shown in such a way that
his supreme Magisterium is acknowledged with reverence
and that the judgments made by him are sincerely adhered
to, according to his manifest mind and will.

Now it should be clear from the reference to the authentic
magisterium of the pope "even when he is not speaking *ex cathedra*," that this text is talking about non-infallible teaching. But
in case that isn't clear, let me direct your attention to the official
notes on this text provided by the Theological Commission at
Vatican II in order to explain its meaning to the bishops before
they voted on it. When this particular paragraph was added to
the second draft of the schema on the Church, the explanation
was that it had been added "in order to further determine which
assent ought to be given to the teaching of the authentic Magisterium *below the grade of infallibility*."[255] Again, in the third draft,
the paragraph was relocated with the explanation that this was
because "it seemed better to treat of the *non-infallible magisterium
of the Roman pontiff* in the context of the magisterium of the
whole episcopal body."[256]

There should be no doubt, therefore, that when we are talking
about the authentic magisterium of the pope, we are not talking
about infallible teaching. The pope is infallible only when he

---

[255] *Acta Synodalia Sacrosancti Concilii Vaticani II*, 2/1, p. 255; emphasis
added.
[256] Ibid., 3/1, p. 250.

speaks *ex cathedra*. And that is usually referred to as his solemn or extraordinary magisterium, not his merely authentic magisterium.

However, in case that is not clear enough, let me add a second proof from Pope John Paul II's Catechesis on the Church. In his general audience of March 24, 1993, he clearly and explicitly asserts that the pope speaks infallibly "only [*solo*] when he speaks *ex cathedra*." Now we have it from *Lumen Gentium* 25 that the pope exercises his authentic magisterium "even when not speaking *ex cathedra*." So if he is infallible *only* when he speaks *ex cathedra*, then he is not infallible when he does not speak *ex cathedra*, even if he is exercising his authentic magisterium.

Here is another dilemma for anyone who thinks that the authentic magisterium of the pope cannot teach error: John Paul II was exercising his authentic magisterium in the general audience mentioned above, but it certainly didn't meet the requirements for speaking *ex cathedra*. So either John Paul II was right and the pope is not infallible in his authentic magisterium when not speaking *ex cathedra*, or he was wrong. But if one were to argue that he was wrong, then it would mean that he taught something false in his authentic magisterium. In other words, his own error would prove that he was right after all. No matter which way you slice it, the conclusion necessarily follows that popes can teach error in their authentic magisterium when they are not speaking *ex cathedra*.

Let me insert a brief logic lesson here for the 2+2 = 5 crowd. If it's not infallible, then it's fallible. And if it's fallible, then it could be in error. Deny that and you may as well walk right through the door marked *"Abandon Reason All Ye Who Enter Here."*

Now all of this has to be borne in mind in order to understand what is really required by a "religious submission (*obsequio*) of will and intellect" to the teaching of the authentic magisterium of the pope or of the bishops.

Normally, of course, it means that the teaching in question should be accepted as true, though with the awareness that it could be false. In the scholastic terminology this is the kind of assent characteristic of *opinions* rather than *knowledge*. When I say *I know* that something is true, my assent is certain. When I say *I think* that something is true, my assent is given, but without certainty and with a recognition of the possibility of error.

Due to the assistance of the Holy Spirit given to the Church, we can be sure that instances of error in this kind of authentic teaching are rare. And yet since they are possible, our response must also take that into account. So what does the obligation of religious submission mean for Catholics in individual cases of teaching from the authentic magisterium? I think it can be summed up best by saying that we should accept that teaching as true precisely to the extent that it does not conflict with irreformable Catholic doctrine.

3

Capital Punishment and the Infallibility of the Church

In a two-part essay at *Public Discourse*,[257] E. Christian Brugger has responded to Edward Feser and Joseph M. Bessette's *By Man Shall His Blood Be Shed: A Catholic Defense of Capital Punishment* (San Francisco: Ignatius Press, 2017). Feser and Bessette argue that the Church's traditional teaching on the moral permissibility of the death penalty is irreformable and that it is therefore illegitimate—indeed, "close to heresy"—for any Catholic to assert that the death penalty is *intrinsically* wrong (they allow that Catholics may legitimately disagree about the prudence of employing the death penalty in any particular circumstances). Brugger claims that they are wrong; and that capital punishment *is* intrinsically wrong. But he is wrong.

In his response to Feser and Bessette, Brugger attempts to show that the Church has never *infallibly* taught that capital punishment is morally permissible in principle. But in order to do so he relies on an excessively narrow conception of the ordinary

---

[257] "Capital Punishment Is Intrinsically Wrong: A Reply to Feser and Bessette" and "Catholic Tradition, St. John Paul II, and the Death Penalty," October 22 and 23, 2017, www.thepublicdiscourse.com/2017/10/20341/ and www.thepublicdiscourse.com/2017/10/20344/.

magisterium. Brugger relies on the text of *Lumen Gentium* 25 in setting out what he takes to be four necessary conditions for the infallible exercise of the ordinary and universal magisterium and argues that the traditional teaching of the Church regarding the morality of the death penalty fails to meet any of them. (Really? The bishops have never maintained the bond of communion among themselves and with the successor of Peter?) The text he cites is this (with his enumeration):

> Although the individual bishops do not enjoy the preroga-
> tive of infallibility, they nevertheless proclaim Christ's doc-
> trine infallibly whenever, even though dispersed through
> the world, but still (1) maintaining the bond of communion
> among themselves and with the successor of Peter, and
> (2) authentically teaching matters of faith and morals, (3)
> they are in agreement on one position (4) as definitively
> to be held.

But, Brugger claims, not many bishops have ever *authentically* taught the legitimacy of the death penalty, and only very few taught this as a doctrine that must be *definitively held*. Regardless of the truth of these claims, however, Brugger's fundamental mistake is to assume that the infallible teaching of the ordinary and universal magisterium can be found only in the explicit statements of the bishops.

Admittedly, one could easily come to such a conclusion from reading this text in isolation, but the fact is that the ordinary and universal magisterium encompasses much more than this.

The Origins of the Term "Ordinary Magisterium"
The term "ordinary magisterium" came to prominence through the writings of Joseph Kleutgen, a neo-scholastic Jesuit theologian

of the middle of the nineteenth century. He was concerned to combat the tendency of many modern theologians (especially in Germany) to assume that if a doctrine had not been defined by a judgment of the Church, it was a matter of free opinion. Against this idea, he wanted to reassert the fundamental authority of Scripture and Tradition against an excessive reliance on only the explicit judgments of the Church. But he also wanted to uphold the Catholic principle of ecclesiastical mediation against the Protestant principle of private interpretation. His solution was to describe the living tradition itself as a mode of exercise of the magisterium. The term "ordinary magisterium" is not meant to describe a certain kind of magisterial document. It is meant to describe the living tradition itself, and especially meant to highlight the authoritative nature of the Church's transmission of divine revelation apart from and in addition to the explicit magisterial statements of the hierarchy.

In proof of the authority of the living tradition/ordinary magisterium, Kleutgen appeals to the practice of the ancient Fathers of the Church, who did not hesitate to accuse Marcion, Arius, Nestorius, and many others of heresy even before their doctrines had been condemned by a judgment of the Church; in fact, it was precisely this vigorous opposition that eventually led to their formal condemnation. Yet how could this be if the faith of the Church were unable to be known with certitude apart from her formal judgments? The Fathers of the Church who opposed Arius, for example, seem to have acted on the assumption that the co-equal divinity of Father and Son was sufficiently taught by the Church such that its denial constituted heresy even prior to its solemn definition at the First Council of Nicaea. In Kleutgen's terminology, it was already infallibly proposed as a dogma of faith by the ordinary magisterium prior to its solemn definition by the extraordinary magisterium. And the Fathers of the Church were not gathering citations from the authentic teaching documents of every bishop dispersed throughout the world. They were citing the clear teaching of Scripture and the Tradition received from the apostles.

Identifying the Teaching of the Ordinary Magisterium

The teaching of the ordinary magisterium may be seen in many places, but most clearly in Scripture itself. Kleutgen writes:

> The Church, initially through her constant and ordinary magisterium, subsequently also through explicit conciliar definitions, has declared that the Holy Scriptures, as we have them now, are the genuine and unadulterated word of God. Thus she has also proposed to us for belief their entire contents as the revelation of God. Therefore, as soon as we cannot doubt that something is contained in the Scriptures, so we are also certain that this is taught by the Church as revealed truth.[258]

And even for those passages in Scripture which are not sufficiently clear in themselves, says Kleutgen, the Council of Trent refers the faithful not to the explicit judgments of the Church but to "that meaning which she has always held and holds" and to "the unanimous interpretation of the Fathers," or in other words, to the living tradition.

So when Kleutgen says that Catholics are bound not only by the extraordinary magisterium but also by the infallible teaching of the ordinary magisterium, he means that Catholics are bound not only by the formal judgments of the Church, but also by the

---

[258] *Die Theologie der Vorzeit*, 1st ed., 49.

word of God itself handed down in the Church through her living tradition. In addition to the plain sense of Scripture, therefore, one ought to look for the teaching of the ordinary magisterium in the teaching of the Fathers, who are the privileged witnesses of the Church's tradition, and then also in the writings of other prominent doctors and theologians, the monuments of antiquity (e.g., graves with their inscriptions, churches with their altars and paintings), the customs, laws, and liturgies of the Church, and the decrees of individual bishops and local councils.[259] In other words, the teaching of the ordinary magisterium is to be sought in all the traditional *loci theologici*; and the statements of individual bishops comes only at the end of the list.

Finally, because the investigation of all the sources of theology may often be long and arduous, Kleutgen also proposes "a short and easy path for recognizing, even in difficult cases, whether something belongs to the general faith of the Church."[260] This is the unanimous consensus of the most prestigious theologians. His basic claim is that, when all the most prestigious theologians agree that something is a dogma of faith, even though not determined by a solemn judgment of the Church, they are witnesses of the fact that it belongs to the general faith of the Church. And although the theologians themselves are certainly not infallible, "their testimony, when it is so explicit and unanimous, must be held as unobjectionable."[261]

As examples of dogmas never defined by explicit judgment but taught infallibly by the ordinary magisterium, Kleutgen includes: that Christians have the moral duty to love their neighbors; that

---

[259] Ibid., 51.
[260] Ibid., 57.
[261] Ibid., 58.

pride is a sin and humility a virtue; that God is infinite according to His nature, that He is all good and all knowing, that He foresees the free actions of men; that He freely created and rules the world; that creatures not only receive their existence from Him, but are also held in being by Him; that His providence extends over everything; that the fallen angels are all damned; and that the souls in purgatory are unable to grow in virtue and merit.

Are we unable to present all eight beatitudes with confidence as doctrines of our Lord or must we choose only those few which are partially reflected in judgments of the Church? Can we not present the flight of our Lord to Egypt as part of the faith with as much confidence as His birth and crucifixion? May we not believe in the sending of the Holy Spirit on Pentecost and our Lord's prior promise of this sending just as we believe in the divinity of the Holy Spirit as divinely revealed truths? According to Kleutgen, we can, and indeed, we must.

By Brugger's standards, all of these doctrines would be up for grabs.

Vatican I on the Ordinary Magisterium

Kleutgen's use of the term "ordinary magisterium" was soon picked up and introduced into the official vocabulary of the Church by Pope Pius IX in the apostolic letter *Tuas Libenter* (1863) and then by Vatican I in the constitution on the Catholic faith *Dei Filius* (1870). The influence of Kleutgen on these documents is clear not only from their contents, but also from the historical records in the Vatican Archives. Kleutgen was even directly involved in the drafting of *Dei Filius* as a *peritus* at the council. His influence is most clearly felt in ch. 3, which states: "Wherefore, by divine and Catholic faith all those things are to be believed which are contained in the word of God as found in Scripture and tradition, and which are proposed by the Church as matters to be believed as divinely revealed, whether by her solemn judgment or in her ordinary and universal magisterium."

When this text came up for discussion at the First Vatican Council it was met with some opposition. Several bishops objected that it should be moved to the schema on the Church instead of that on the Catholic faith. One bishop argued that it was simply false because doctrines taught by the ordinary magisterium are *not* to be believed with Catholic faith. Many bishops objected (prophetically, as it turns out) that the term "ordinary magisterium" is obscure and ambiguous. The only bishop to voice support for the text initially was one who thought the term "ordinary magisterium" was meant to be understood in reference to the papal magisterium (a misunderstanding which was then urged by others as further proof of the obscurity and ambiguity of the term).

Bishop Martin of Paderborn intervened on behalf of the deputation responsible for drafting the text in order to respond to these objections. He defended the use of the novel term "ordinary magisterium" by pointing out that it had already been used by Pope Pius IX in *Tuas Libenter*.

After this, several more bishops commented (more approvingly) on the text and expressed their understanding of the ordinary magisterium in various ways as consisting in the daily preaching, liturgical prayers, method of conducting and defining business in the episcopal courts, and in the Roman congregations; as being exercised under the authority of the hierarchy, through pastors and teachers, through bishops and parish priests, through the words of preachers, through orthodox theologians, through approved books, through liturgical books and catechisms, etc.

Granted, none of this detail enters into the final text of *Dei Filius*, nor is the meaning of the term "ordinary magisterium" explained in any more detail in *Tuas Libenter*, and it is not even used in the text of *Lumen Gentium*, which is Brugger's only source. The fact is that the Church has offered very little explicit clarification of the term "ordinary magisterium" even while insisting on its authority. But it is sufficiently clear that the way in which it was used and intended to be understood by Pius IX and the First Vatican Council (which are cited in a footnote on the relevant passage of *Lumen Gentium* together with a commentary by Kleutgen himself) is quite a far cry from Brugger's more limited notion of the ordinary magisterium consisting exclusively in the explicit magisterial statements of the bishops.

What Feser and Bessette have done in their work on capital punishment is to build an impressive case for the irreformability of the Church's traditional teaching by amassing evidence of the teaching of the ordinary magisterium in all its dimensions. To argue that not much of this evidence comes from explicit magisterial statements of bishops is beside the point.

4

The Magisterial Weight of the New Text of the Catechism on the Death Penalty

In view of the uproar caused by Pope Francis's decision to alter the text of the Catechism on the death penalty, it may be helpful to pause and consider the magisterial weight or degree of teaching authority exercised by the pope in promulgating this text and the corresponding response due to this teaching on the part of the faithful. The three levels of magisterial authority are outlined in the concluding formula of the Profession of Faith as follows:

> With firm faith, I also believe everything contained in the word of God, whether written or handed down in Tradition, which the Church, either by a solemn judgment or by the ordinary and universal Magisterium, sets forth to be believed as divinely revealed.
>
> I also firmly accept and hold each and everything definitively proposed by the Church regarding teaching on faith and morals.
>
> Moreover, I adhere with religious submission of will and intellect to the teachings which either the Roman Pontiff or the College of Bishops enunciate when they exercise their authentic Magisterium, even if they do not intend to proclaim these teachings by a definitive act.[262]

[262] Congregation for the Doctrine of the Faith, *Professio fidei* (1998).

The first two paragraphs refer to the infallible teaching of the Church, which is proposed either as contained in divine revelation and so "to be believed as divinely revealed" (first paragraph) or as at least connected to divine revelation and so "definitively to be held" (second paragraph). The third paragraph refers to the authentic (that is, authoritative) but not infallible teaching of the pope or bishops.

The pope teaches infallibly only when he fulfills the requirements set forth by the First Vatican Council.[263] These requirements are essentially three, pertaining to the subject, object, and act of the teaching.[264] (1) On the part of the subject, the pope must be speaking as supreme head of the universal Church and not merely as a private person or a local bishop; (2) on the part of the object, the pope must be speaking about a matter of faith or morals; (3) and on the part of the act itself, the pope must define the doctrine by a definitive act.[265]

---

[263] Vatican I, *Pastor Aeternus*, cap. 4: "When the Roman Pontiff speaks *ex cathedra*, that is, when, in the exercise of his office as shepherd and teacher of all Christians, in virtue of his supreme apostolic authority, he defines a doctrine concerning faith or morals to be held by the whole Church, he possesses, by the divine assistance promised to him in blessed Peter, that infallibility which the divine Redeemer willed his Church to enjoy in defining doctrine concerning faith or morals."

[264] See *The Gift of Infallibility: The Official Relatio on Infallibility of Bishop Vincent Gasser at Vatican Council I*, trans. James T. O'Connor (Boston: St. Paul Editions, 1986), 45–46.

[265] Cf. Vatican II, *Lumen Gentium*, 25: "And this is the infallibility which the Roman Pontiff, the head of the college of bishops, enjoys in virtue of his office, when, as the supreme shepherd and teacher of all the faithful, who confirms his brethren in their faith (Lk 22:32), by a definitive act he proclaims a doctrine of faith or morals."

Magisterial Weight of the New Text of the Catechism

In the present case, there is no great difficulty in recognizing that Pope Francis was acting in an official capacity as supreme head of the Church when he approved the new text of the Catechism n. 2267 and ordered it to be inserted into all editions of the *Catechism of the Catholic Church*, which is intended as a teaching document for the whole Church. And there seems to be no doubt that the text in question has to do with matters of faith and morals, for the death penalty pertains in itself to morals and the teaching is proposed explicitly "in the light of the Gospel"[266] and in the context of an exposition of the Fifth Commandment. But with respect to the third requirement, there does not seem to be any evidence of the definitive mode of proclamation that is required for infallibility. The burden of proof would in any case be on anyone who wanted to assert that it does constitute an infallible definition.[267]

But just because it is not infallible does not mean that it is not authoritative. The conditions for authoritative (or authentic) papal teaching are less stringent than for infallible papal teaching. For authentic papal teaching it is enough for the pope, acting in an official capacity as pope, to propose a teaching regarding faith or morals even if not by a definitive act. The rescript, therefore, by which the new text of the Catechism on the death penalty was published on August 2, 2018, is an act of the authentic papal magisterium, which calls for a religious submission of will and intellect on the part of all the faithful.[268]

---

[266] "New Redaction of n. 2267 of the *Catechism of the Catholic Church* on the Death Penalty," August 2, 2018.

[267] CIC 749, §3: "No doctrine is understood as defined infallibly unless this is manifestly evident."

[268] Vatican II, *Lumen Gentium*, 25: "This religious submission of mind and will must be shown in a special way to the authentic

Religious Submission of Will and Intellect

The nature of this religious submission of will and intellect corresponds to the nature of the authentic but non-definitive magisterium: because the teaching is authoritative, it calls for a genuine internal assent; but because the teaching is not definitive, the nature of the assent will be provisional. In other words, it will have more the character of opinion rather than knowledge, since the doctrine is to be accepted as true, though with the awareness that it could possibly be false.[269]

However, although this religious submission is normally due to the teaching of the authentic magisterium, it may legitimately be withheld in certain cases.[270] To do so merely on the basis of one's own private judgment would certainly be rash and dangerous, but assent must be withheld when the teaching in question openly conflicts with the public dogma or definitive doctrine of the Church. For in the case of conflicting obligations, precedence must always be given to the stricter obligation; and the obligation to give definitive assent to the irreformable doctrines of the infallible Church is a stricter obligation than the religious submission due to the non-infallible teaching of the authentic magisterium. (And it is not possible to assent simultaneously to contradictory propositions.)

---

magisterium of the Roman Pontiff, even when he is not speaking *ex cathedra*; that is, it must be shown in such a way that his supreme magisterium is acknowledged with reverence, the judgments made by him are sincerely adhered to, according to his manifest mind and will."

[269] Cf. St. Thomas Aquinas, *De Veritate*, q. 14, a. 1.

[270] This is discussed by the CDF in *Donum Veritatis* (1990), 24–31.

Magisterial Weight of the Traditional Catholic Teaching

Now the traditional teaching of the Catholic Church is that the death penalty is in principle legitimate,[271] which means that it is not intrinsically immoral. And this traditional teaching is absolutely unchangeable, for it is a dogma of divine and catholic faith.[272]

A dogma is a doctrine contained in divine revelation (Scripture or Tradition) which has been proposed as such by the Church, either by a solemn judgment or by the ordinary and universal

---

[271] See, for example, the *Catechism of the Council of Trent*: "Another kind of lawful slaying belongs to the civil authorities, to whom is entrusted power of life and death, by the legal and judicious exercise of which they punish the guilty and protect the innocent. The just use of this power, far from involving the crime of murder, is an act of paramount obedience to this Commandment which prohibits murder. The end of the Commandment is the preservation and security of human life. Now the punishments inflicted by the civil authority, which is the legitimate avenger of crime, naturally tend to this end, since they give security to life by repressing outrage and violence. Hence these words of David: 'In the morning I put to death all the wicked of the land, that I might cut off all the workers of iniquity from the city of the Lord' (Ps 101:8)."

[272] Vatican I, *Dei Filius*, cap. 4: "That meaning of the sacred dogmas is ever to be maintained which has once been declared by holy mother Church, and there must never be any abandonment of this sense under the pretext or in the name of a more profound understanding. May understanding, knowledge and wisdom increase as ages and centuries roll along, and greatly and vigorously flourish, in each and all, in the individual and the whole Church: but this only in its own proper kind, that is to say, in the same doctrine, the same sense, and the same understanding." Cf. *Dei Filius*, cap. 4, can. 3: "If anyone says that it is possible that at some time, given the advancement of knowledge, a sense may be assigned to the dogmas propounded by the Church which is different from that which the Church has understood and understands: let him be anathema."

magisterium.[273] Now the legitimacy in principle of the death penalty is clearly taught in Scripture. For example: "Whoever sheds the blood of man, by man shall his blood be shed; for God made man in his own image" (Gen 9:6).[274] Nor may any Catholic legitimately dispute this interpretation of Scripture, for the Fathers and Doctors of the Church are unanimous in interpreting Scripture (especially Gen 9:6 and Rom 13:4) as affirming the legitimacy in principle of the death penalty as a matter of justice.[275] And it is never permitted for any Catholic to interpret Scripture contrary to the unanimous consensus of the Fathers, as the Councils of Trent and Vatican I have declared.[276] Moreover,

---

[273] Cf. Vatican, *Dei Filius*, cap. 3: "Wherefore, by divine and catholic faith all those things are to be believed which are contained in the word of God as found in Scripture or tradition, and which are proposed by the Church as matters to be believed as divinely revealed, whether by her solemn judgment or in her ordinary and universal magisterium."

[274] See also Rom 13:1–4; Acts 5:1–11; Acts 25:11; John 19:10–11; and the many crimes for which God required the death penalty to be applied in the law of Moses.

[275] For a thorough review of the evidence of this consensus, see Edward Feser and Joseph Bessette, *By Man Shall His Blood Be Shed: A Catholic Defense of Capital Punishment* (Ignatius Press, 2017); see also Avery Card. Dulles, "Catholicism and Capital Punishment," *First Things* (April 2001).

[276] Vatican I, *Dei Filius*, cap. 2: "In matters of faith and morals, belonging as they do to the establishing of Christian doctrine, that meaning of Holy Scripture must be held to be the true one, which Holy Mother Church held and holds, since it is her right to judge of the true meaning and interpretation of Holy Scripture. In consequence, it is not permissible for anyone to interpret Holy Scripture in a sense contrary to this, or indeed against the unanimous consensus of the Fathers." Cf. Council of Trent, *Second Decree on Scripture*.

such a unanimous consensus is sufficient proof that the doctrine has been infallibly taught by the magisterium of the Church dispersed throughout the world.[277] Therefore, the legitimacy in principle of the death penalty as a matter of justice is a dogma of divine and catholic faith. And to doubt or deny a dogma of divine and catholic faith is heresy.[278]

What Does This Mean for the New Text of the Catechism?

The new text of the Catechism n. 2267 reads as follows:

> Recourse to the death penalty on the part of legitimate authority, following a fair trial, was long considered an appropriate response to the gravity of certain crimes and an acceptable, albeit extreme, means of safeguarding the common good.
>
> Today, however, there is an increasing awareness that the dignity of the person is not lost even after the commission of very serious crimes. In addition, a new understanding has emerged of the significance of penal sanctions imposed by the state. Lastly, more effective systems of detention have been developed, which ensure the due protection of citizens but, at the same time, do not definitively deprive the guilty of the possibility of redemption.
>
> Consequently, the Church teaches, in the light of the Gospel, that "the death penalty is inadmissible because it is an attack on the inviolability and dignity of the person", and she works with determination for its abolition worldwide.[279]

---

[277] Cf. Pope Pius IX, *Tuas Libenter*; Vatican I, *Dei Filius*, cap. 3.

[278] CIC 751.

[279] "New Redaction of n. 2267 of the *Catechism of the Catholic Church* on the Death Penalty," August 2, 2018.

In the letter from the Congregation for the Doctrine of the Faith to the bishops regarding this new revision, Cardinal Ladaria asserts that this teaching constitutes "an authentic development of doctrine that is not in contradiction with the prior teachings of the Magisterium,"[280] which can only means that it does not deny the legitimacy in principle of the death penalty. He also acknowledges that, "the political and social situation of the past [may have] made the death penalty an acceptable means for the protection of the common good,"[281] which seems to suggest that this text is not intended to be understood as meaning that the death penalty is intrinsically immoral. For anything that is intrinsically immoral can never be justified under any circumstances, past, present, or future. Moreover, the development of more effective prisons in modern society is cited as one of the reasons for the new teaching, which would seem to allow for the fact that the death penalty could have been justified prior to the development of better prisons, in which case, presumably, it can still be justified in less developed societies, and could be justified again if the prison systems in more developed societies deteriorate. And anything that could ever be justified cannot be intrinsically immoral.

On the other hand, to say that the death penalty is inadmissible precisely "because it is an attack on the inviolability and dignity of the person" is hard to understand in any other way than as an assertion of its intrinsic immorality. For surely it is always and everywhere immoral to attack the inviolability and dignity of the person. Likewise, the earlier remark of Pope Francis cited in the

---

[280] CDF, "Letter to the Bishops regarding the new revision of number 2267 of the *Catechism of the Catholic Church* on the death penalty," August 1, 2018, n. 1.
[281] Ibid., 2.

letter to the bishops: "The death penalty, regardless of the means of execution, 'entails cruel, inhumane, and degrading treatment.'"[282] For again, it is surely always and everywhere immoral to treat people in a manner that is cruel, inhumane, and degrading.

It is hard to avoid the conclusion, therefore, that this text suffers from serious ambiguity (inasmuch as it seems to be open to multiple interpretations) or even incoherence (inasmuch as it seems to assert contradictory propositions). In any case, however, Catholics are obliged to continue believing that the death penalty is in principle legitimate, since this is a dogma of divine and catholic faith; and because of the religious submission of will and intellect due to the authentic magisterium of the Holy Father, Catholics should also refrain from interpreting the new text of the Catechism in a manner that would contradict the traditional dogma as long as any other interpretation remains possible.

---

[282] Ibid., 6. Citing Pope Francis, "Letter to the President of the International Commission against the Death Penalty," March 20, 2015, in *L'Osservatore Romano* (March 20–21, 2015), 7.

5

The Pope Is Not the Church and the Church Is Not the Pope

In 1967, the Congregation for the Doctrine of the Faith introduced a new formula to be used in place of the Tridentine Profession of Faith and the Oath against Modernism in all cases where those used to be required. This was updated in 1988 and then re-promulgated again in 1998. The current version consists of the Nicene Creed followed by three concluding paragraphs, as given at the start of the preceding chapter (see page 143: "With firm faith ...")

Although greatly lacking in doctrinal content compared to the Tridentine Profession and the Anti-Modernist Oath, these three paragraphs do provide a very helpful and concise outline of the various degrees of authority and modes of exercise of the magisterium. The first paragraph is about the infallible dogmas of the Church; the second paragraph deals with non-dogmatic but still infallible doctrines of the Church; whereas the third paragraph treats of the non-infallible teaching of the pope and bishops.

One point that is easy to overlook, however, is the shift in terminology between the first two paragraphs (infallible teaching) and the third paragraph (non-infallible teaching). In the first two cases, it is "the Church" who teaches. The pope and bishops are not mentioned until the third paragraph. Why the shift? The teaching activity of the pope and the bishops is clearly implied in the first two paragraphs. The solemn judgments mentioned in the first paragraph refer to *ex cathedra* definitions of popes and solemn definitions of ecumenical councils of bishops; the teaching of the ordinary and universal magisterium refers to the common teaching of the bishops dispersed throughout the world. In these cases, when the pope and bishops teach infallibly, their teaching is attributed to the Church; but when they are not teaching infallibly, their teaching is attributed to themselves. The Church as such drops out of the picture.

Why Is This Important?

According to the Catechism of the Council of Trent, "[The] Church cannot err in faith or morals, since it is guided by the Holy Ghost" (Part I, a. 9). Similarly, the Baltimore Catechism says, "The Church cannot err when it teaches a doctrine of faith or morals" (no. 526). In the words of the blessed Apostle Paul, the Church is "the pillar and bulwark of the truth" (1 Tim 3:15), as well as the immaculate bride of Christ, "without spot or wrinkle or any such thing … holy and without blemish" (Eph 5:27).

The Church is infallible. The Church is holy. The Church is guided by the Holy Spirit. But have you ever heard someone (or caught yourself) saying, "The Church" did or said something, when in fact it was the pope who did or said that thing? One of the common symptoms of hyperpapalism is a tendency to identify the pope with the Church, or to identify papal teaching with Church teaching as if the two were entirely synonymous.

False Identification

Once you accept a total identification of the pope and the Church, you start expecting every pope to be a pure and holy pillar of truth in the same absolute sense. This kind of identification happens even at lower levels of the hierarchy. When your neighbor says that she has been hurt by "the Church," what she really means is that she has been hurt by some member of the clergy. This false identification is especially tempting and problematic with the pope because he is the visible head of the Church on earth, and so he *can* in some cases speak and act for the Church—*in persona Ecclesiae*, as it were. But most of his acts do not fall in that category.

When it comes to teaching in matters of faith and morals, the pope speaks for the Church only when he speaks *ex cathedra*, and when he does that, he *does* possess the full infallibility of the Church. But in every other case—whether in encyclical letters, post-synodal apostolic exhortations, paragraphs of the catechism, letters to bishops accompanying liturgical legislation, and so on and so forth—he speaks only on his own authority as the pope. In such cases, we should not say that "the Church" teaches something, but rather that the pope teaches it; and thus if he were to err in his teaching, we would say that the pope has erred and not that the Church has erred.

For example, when the medieval Pope John XXII taught in some papal sermons that the souls of the saints do not see the vision of God until after the final judgment, Catholics did not conclude that this novel doctrine was now "Church teaching." Quite the contrary, many Catholic theologians at the time, including Cardinal Jacques Fournier (who as Pope Benedict XII would later condemn this novel teaching as heretical), knew that "the Church" actually believed the opposite and so concluded quite simply that the pope was wrong.

Submission to the Non-Infallible Papal Magisterium Is Conditional

So far, I have made the case that the pope, when he exercises his non-infallible teaching authority, as he typically does in encyclical letters, apostolic exhortations, letters to bishops, etc., does not speak therein with the full authority of the Church (as he does when he speaks *ex cathedra*), but rather with his own authority as the pope.

This authority, however, which the pope exercises even when not speaking infallibly, is still considerable. The obligation to accept non-infallible papal teaching has been forcefully expressed in many authoritative documents. For example, Pope Pius XII, in *Humani Generis* §20, says this: "Nor must it be thought that what is expounded in encyclical letters does not of itself demand assent, since in writing such letters the popes do not exercise the supreme power of their teaching authority." Vatican II, in *Lumen Gentium* §25, puts it this way:

> In matters of faith and morals, the bishops speak in the name of Christ and the faithful are to accept their teaching and adhere to it with a religious assent. This religious submission of mind and will must be shown in a special way to the authentic magisterium of the Roman Pontiff, even when he is not speaking *ex cathedra*; that is, it must be shown in such a way that his supreme magisterium is acknowledged with reverence, the judgments made by him are sincerely adhered to, according to his manifest mind and will.

If even the non-infallible teaching of popes and bishops requires "religious assent" or "religious submission of will and intellect," it might be tempting to conclude that the distinction between infallible and non-infallible papal teaching is merely academic. If a faithful Catholic is obliged to accept all of it in any case, then there would not seem to be much practical difference between the infallible teaching and the authentic (non-infallible) teaching.

But what exactly is this religious assent? It must correspond in nature to the kind of teaching to which it responds; that is, teaching which is *authoritative* but *not infallible*. Because it is authoritative, we owe it our assent; but because it is not infallible, this assent must be opinionative and conditional in nature.

By *opinionative*, I mean that if a pope officially teaches something about faith or morals in a non-infallible way, then we are obliged to *think* that what he teaches is true (while still acknowledging that it could be false). This is typical of the way we express opinions: I *think* that the Detroit Tigers will not win the World Series this year (even though I know they could). This is a real assent—I really do think that the Tigers will not win and I have good reason for thinking that; but it is the kind of assent characteristic of opinions rather than certain knowledge.

The religious assent due to non-infallible papal teaching is also *conditional*. By that, I mean that the obligation holds only as long as it does not conflict with a higher obligation. This is typical of basic moral reasoning in any case where different obligations come into conflict with one another. The obligation to obey the speed limit, for example, might give way in certain cases to a higher obligation to get a dying person to the hospital in time to save his life. The obligation not to break into a neighbor's house will give way to the higher obligation to save a life if someone is trapped inside when the house is on fire.

An even better example to illustrate the point under discussion is the way we teach the fourth commandment to children. We ordinarily express the obligation that children should obey their parents in an unqualified way, as St. Paul does to the Ephesians: "Children, obey your parents in the Lord, for this is just" (Eph 6:1); but this command is always understood to be conditional rather than absolute. It applies only on the condition that parents act within the scope of their authority under divine and natural law. Were a parent to command something contrary to a higher law (divine or natural), then the child's obligation to obey his parent would cease in that case. For "we ought to obey God, rather than men," as St. Peter says (Acts 5:29).

Similarly, we are obliged to accept the non-infallible teaching of our Holy Father only on the condition that he acts within the scope of his authority under divine law. If he were to teach something contrary to a higher law of belief, then the obligation to give religious assent to this teaching would yield to the stricter obligation binding the faithful to believe the word of God and hold fast to the infallible teaching of the Church.

Appendix

On Non-infallible Teachings of the Magisterium and the Meaning of *Obsequium Religiosum*

Jeremy Holmes
Associate Professor of Theology
Wyoming Catholic College

Pope Francis's many controversial statements have brought with them a new interest in how Catholics should respond to non-infallible teachings of the Magisterium. The pope's infallibility was only solemnly defined in the late nineteenth century, so it is no surprise that careful reflection on non-infallible-but-still-authoritative teachings is a fairly recent thing. Vatican II's constitution *Lumen Gentium* tackles the topic head-on, but even there it just says that we owe the pope's non-infallible statements a religious *obsequium* of mind and will. This language was picked up in the Catechism of the Catholic Church, Canon Law, the CDF's Instruction on the Ecclesial Vocation of the Theologian, the *Professio fidei*, and the CDF's doctrinal commentary on the concluding formula of the *Professio fidei*, so it appears to be the Church's phrasing of choice for describing a Catholic's proper response to non-infallible magisterial teaching in general.

But what does it mean? Sometimes "religious *obsequium*" is translated "religious assent," at other times "religious submission," and at other times "religious respect." What exactly are we being asked to do? Taking into account everything said in the above-mentioned documents, and looking a bit deeper for a theological account of what they say, let's unpack the key term *obsequium*.

The Dictionary Meaning of the Word

The Latin word *obsequium* is not a mystery in itself. Its basic meaning is compliance or a readiness to comply.[283] So for example, the Roman army would bring a people back to *obsequium*—that is, subjugate them—by force of arms. Or a lover would show *obsequium*—a readiness to, erm, "comply" with her man. In English we have an old-but-not-quite obsolete word "obsequy" to signify the same thing. In the context of theology, the meaning of *obsequium* is admirably captured by the English word "submission."

As the above examples show, to call something *obsequium* is a fairly outward description of what is going on: the interior motivation behind the *obsequium* could be almost anything. One complies with one's lover out of amorous love. One has a readiness to comply to the Roman army because they kill disobedient people. One complies with the commands of one's parents out of respect for them as parents—or perhaps for fear of a spanking. One complies with the government's laws both because they are the custodians of the common good (reverence) and because they can punish (fear). In some of these cases the *obsequium* is a moral obligation, while in others it is just a fact arising from the situation. When someone's readiness to comply is driven by flattery, such that he changes with every slightest perceived whim of his master, we call him "obsequious."

---

[283] So the Oxford Latin Dictionary, which also offers as extended meanings "assiduous service or attention," "deference," or "solicitude."

The *obsequium* we give to the Magisterium is specified as "religious": it does not arise from fear for our lives, nor from amorous love, but from reverence.

Reverence for what? For the office, bestowed on certain men by God, of protecting the Church's common good, a common good that includes the truth of the faith. We meet a teaching from the Magisterium with an act of submission (*obsequium*) inspired by reverence for the Magisterium's God-given office (*religiosum*). It is like the reverence one has for a sacred place: one would not carry out a non-religious activity in a Church without a pressing reason; one would be even more reluctant to transgress the sanctuary itself except in a case of great necessity; one would never in any situation agree to strike a monstrance or a tabernacle or do anything else that would endanger the Eucharist; and one could not conceive of disrespecting the Eucharist itself. The reverence due to the sacred forbids it.

To refuse assent to a magisterial teaching is to transgress the Magisterium's sacred office, while to assent is to act with reverence toward it. This is why some translations of *Lumen Gentium* render the word *obsequium* as "respect." Although this is a decent attempt to describe the nature of the act, the English word "respect" seems to fall somewhat short of the strong reverence due to a sacred office, and it reaches for one of the more extended lexical meanings of the Latin word *obsequium*. For the purposes of this article, I will continue to render *obsequium* as "submission," as better capturing the natural species of the act, while pursuing the idea of "reverence" as expressing the moral species of the act.

Degrees of Engagement of the Magisterium's Authority

While I compared reverence for the Magisterium to reverence for a church or a tabernacle, there is a key difference between reverence for inanimate sacred things and reverence for a sacred person. The sacred thing is simply there, more or less sacred as the Church has made it so. But a person holding a sacred office can choose to bring the sacredness of his office more or less to bear on a situation. So while a church is only as sacred as it is, and the sanctuary inevitably more so, and the tabernacle even more so, a person holding the magisterial office can engage his office to a lesser degree, a greater degree, or a maximal degree, depending on his judgment.

There is nothing mystical about this. Every moral authority works the same way. For example, a child should obey his father out of piety, and the father can invoke his God-given role as father to a greater or a lesser degree. Sometimes the father only interposes his paternal office slightly, and the child knows that a slight reason would be enough to justify transgressing his father's request. At other times the father interposes his paternal office more significantly, so the child knows that it is unlikely any reason would justify disobedience. And sometimes, in rare cases, the father can lay his entire paternal office between the child and a given deed, as though to say: If you do this, you utterly disrespect my paternity. The child who goes ahead with the deed at that point estranges himself from his father.

The same thing is true of governmental authority. While the government has power to punish those who are not motivated by anything more noble than fear, a good citizen obeys the law out of reverence for the office of the lawgiver. And the government indicates the greater and lesser degrees to which it interposes the dignity of its office between a citizen and a given deed by assigning greater and lesser penalties. For something trivial, like a speeding violation, the penalty is trivial. For something that defies all the demands of reverence for lawful authority, like treason, the penalty can even be death.

Notice that neither of these cases depends on the particular expertise of the one who holds the office. It helps if one's father is wise, but piety makes demands even toward a mediocre parent; no one in his right mind presumes the government knows best, but every good citizen intuitively obeys laws promulgated by the legitimate authorities.

Invoking the Office of the Magisterium to Varying Degrees
So it comes as no surprise that those entrusted with guarding the Church's common good, the truth of the faith, can interpose the sacredness of their office between believers and a given path to a greater or lesser degree, even to the point of putting their entire office at stake. When the Magisterium only partially interposes its office between believer and deed, we have non-infallible yet magisterial teachings. When the Magisterium entirely interposes its office between believer and deed, it makes a difference who does this and how:

- If an individual bishop completely interposes his office and the believer goes ahead anyway, he is estranged from that bishop, although not necessarily from the Church. One might have to do this sometimes, if the bishop in question has himself betrayed the office he invokes. This is like the case when a child simply must disobey an abusive father, who has made a mockery of his paternity.
- If the bishops all together, or the bishop of Rome acting as their head, completely interpose their office—not just this man's episcopacy, but the episcopacy as a whole—and one goes ahead, then one is estranged from the Church. Because God gave the episcopacy to the Church, breaking ties with the episcopacy as such can never be a good idea.

• If the bishops all together declare that statement X is in the deposit of revelation, then the case is more serious still. When a person begins to consider whether he should adopt the Christian faith, he hears many different voices: the Bible says things, this and that preacher say things, bishops say things, and even his own experience and random books he picks up. But when he makes the decision that is the act of faith, what he commits to is this: All these many voices were but one voice, the voice of God inviting me to him. His act of faith is an act of hearing the voice of God in obedience. And when the bishops all together, or the pope speaking as their head, declares that a given statement is in the deposit of revelation, their statement merges into the many voices that the believer originally heard and accepted as the voice of God. The believer's response is no longer one of reverence for the office of the Magisterium but of trust in God. To withhold assent at this point would be to void the act of faith itself, to undo one's original commitment. It would no longer be a sin of irreverence toward the Magisterium but of heresy. In the analogy of respect for sacred things given above, this would be like desecrating the Eucharist, the very reason why everything around it is sacred.

Each of the above-mentioned levels of authority has a distinct term to describe it. As regards non-infallible magisterial statements, i.e., lesser interpositions of the office, normal people normally do not have any sufficient reason to transgress the interpositions. So the normal outcome of reverence for the Magisterium is compliance, i.e., assent. This assent does not take the form of saying "I know X is true"—this is for acts of faith or of compliance with the definitive magisterium—but of saying "I think that X is true," using the language of firm opinion. Even though the Magisterium can invoke its office more and less here, yielding varying degrees of moral obligation to comply, the responses to these various degrees do not differ *in kind* and so are all described by the same terms.

When the magisterium completely interposes its office, i.e., hands down a definitive teaching, the response is not in any way uncertain. So the response is not described here as *obsequium religiosum*, but *firmiter tenere*, to "hold firmly," saying not "I think" but "I know."

The response to God's voice is *credo*—I believe.

Obsequium religiosum in Cases of Disagreement

With regard to the lesser interpositions of the Magisterium's office, people can find themselves in a hard situation where a good reason for withholding compliance presents itself. However, the reverence given to non-infallible acts is always the same for the same degree of interposition of the office, even though how one acts on that reverence will depend on other factors like one's academic training, one's responsibility for instructing others, the harmony of the teaching with other magisterial teachings, etc. Disagreeing with a non-infallible teaching does not mean withdrawing that which makes the *obsequium religiosum* a meaningful act: in a given case one may not comply, and yet the reverence that normally drives compliance is still present.

The reverence still present is not an empty form, either, because it still imposes certain limits on one's actions. If necessity forced a soldier to move through a church sanctuary with a rifle, for example, he still would not spit chewing tobacco or write on the walls: his reluctant violation of the space would not eliminate his reverence. And similarly, even when we must disagree with magisterial statements—e.g., when they disagree with other magisterial statements—we do so with sorrow at the necessity and with respect for the office and its holder.

It might seem as though the fact that magisterial statement A disagrees with greater magisterial statement B voids the reverence due to A, because reverence for the magisterium itself outweighs what would have been given to A. But this is not so. Suppose for example that a Catholic saw the Eucharist in danger of desecration in the sanctuary and ran pell-mell through the church and through the sanctuary to prevent the desecration: his religious reverence for the church and the sanctuary would not be diminished by his apparently disrespectful behavior. Quite the contrary: he could reverence the sanctuary *only* by rushing to save the Eucharist, the reality which makes the sanctuary sacred.

And again, none of this is mysterious: it is the way moral authority normally works. If a father has repeated command X time and again, in the most serious terms, and then later gives command Y once casually as the child leaves for school, what does the child do if he finds that obeying Y conflicts with obeying X? He understands that his father has substantially invested his paternal office in X and only slightly in Y, and consequently to obey command Y would be to disrespect his father's very fatherhood, and therefore would constitute "obedience" only in an outward and physical way.

The difference in authority levels is also crucial from the parent's point of view: the father expresses some things more seriously and other things more casually precisely because he wants his child to know which things give way in a crisis and which things do not. Imagine the pressure on a father if he knew that every statement he uttered put his entire paternity at stake. Imagine the constraint he would feel if he knew that every command he gave his child, no matter how small, absolutely bound that child in all circumstances. It would be practically unworkable.

The Magisterium is no different in this regard. Sometimes the Church speaks infallibly, putting her entire office at stake and forcing a Catholic to choose: union with the Church or estrangement? Sometimes the Magisterium invests its office not entirely, but substantially. At other times, the Magisterium puts its office behind a given statement only in a small way. These differing levels of authority are there both for the faithful and for the Magisterium itself, to make its moral authority workable. The pope does not have to suffer the intolerable burden of intending to speak infallibly or being seen as speaking infallibly in every circumstance, no matter how casual his utterance. And in hard circumstances, when choices must be made between teachings of higher authority and teachings of lesser authority, the faithful can know that only assent to those teachings in which the Magisterium's office is more invested is true *obsequium religiosum*.

Bibliography

Ecclesiastical Documents

Acta Apostolicae Sedis. Vatican City: Typis Polyglottis Vaticanis, 1909–.

Acta Synodalia Sacrosancti Concilii Oecumenici Vaticani Secundi. Vatican City: Typis Polyglottis Vaticanis, 1970–1999.

Benedict XV, Pope. *Codex Iuris Canonici.* Vatican City: Typis Polyglottis Vaticanis, 1917.

———. Encyclical Letter *Spiritus Paraclitus* (1920).

Benedict XVI, Pope. Homily for Chrism Mass, April 5, 2012.

Boniface VIII, Pope. Papal Bull *Unam Sanctam* (1302).

Cherubini, Laerzio, ed. *Magnum Bullarium Romanum.* Lyons: Borde and Arnaud, 1692–97.

Clement V, Pope. *Meruit* (1306).

Congregation for the Doctrine of the Faith, Formula to adopt from now on in cases in which the Profession of Faith is prescribed by law in substitution of the Tridentine formula and the oath against modernism (1967).

———. Declaration in Defense of the Catholic Doctrine on the Church *Mysterium Ecclesiae* (1973).

———. Doctrinal Commentary on the Concluding Formula of the Profession of Faith (1998).

———. Instruction *Ardens Felicitatis* (2000).

———. Instruction on the Ecclesial Vocation of the Theologian *Donum Veritatis* (1990).

———. Letter to the Bishops regarding the new revision of number 2267 of the Catechism of the Catholic Church on the death penalty (2018).

———. Profession of Faith (1998).

———. Response to Dubium Concerning *Ordinatio Sacerdotalis* (1995).

Council of Trent. *Decree on the Edition and Use of the Sacred Books* (1546).

———. *Second Decree on Scripture* (1546).

Council of Vatican I. Dogmatic Constitution on the Catholic Faith *Dei Filius* (1870).

———. First Dogmatic Constitution on the Church of Christ *Pastor Aeternus* (1870).

Council of Vatican II. Dogmatic Constitution on Divine Revelation *Dei Verbum* (1965).

———. Dogmatic Constitution on the Church *Lumen Gentium* (1964).

———. Pastoral Constitution on the Church in the Modern World *Gaudium et Spes* (1965).

Francis, Pope. *Catechism of the Catholic Church* (2018).

———. Letter to the President of the International Commission Against the Death Penalty (20 March 2015): *L'Osservatore Romano* (20-21 March 2015).

Gasser, Vincent Ferrer. *The Gift of Infallibility: The Official* Relatio *on Infallibility of Bishop Vincent Ferrer Gasser at Vatican Council I*. Trans. James T. O'Connor. 2nd ed. San Francisco: Ignatius Press, 2008.

Gregory XVI, Pope. Encyclical Letter *Commissum Divinitus* (1835).

Innocent III, Pope. *Apostolicae Sedis Primatus* (1199).

John Paul II, Pope. Address to the Bishops from the United States of America on Their *Ad Limina* Visit, October 15, 1988.

———. Angelus Address, October 1, 2000.

———. Apostolic Letter *Ordinatio Sacerdotalis* (1994).

———. *Catechism of the Catholic Church* (1997).

———. *Codex Iuris Canonici.* Vatican City: Typis Polyglottis Vaticanis, 1983.

———. Encyclical Letter *Evangelium Vitae* (1995).

———. Encyclical Letter *Veritatis Splendor* (1993).

———. General Audience of March 10, 1993.

———. General Audience of March 24, 1993.

———. Motu Proprio *Ad Tuendam Fidem* (1998).

Leo X, Pope. Papal Bull *Exsurge Domine* (1520).

Leo XIII, Pope. Encyclical Letter *Providentissimus Deus* (1893).

Mansi, Giovanni Domenico. *Sacrorum Conciliorum Nova et Amplissima Collectio.* Paris: Welter, 1901–1927.

Paul VI, Pope. Address During the Last General Meeting of the Second Vatican Council, December 7, 1965.

———. Creed of the People of God *Solemni Hac Liturgia* (1968).

———. Encyclical Letter *Humanae Vitae* (1968).

———. General Audience of January 12, 1966.

Pius IX, Pope. Apostolic Letter *Tuas Libenter* (1863).

———. Encyclical Letter *Quanta Cura* (1864).

Pius V, Pope. *Catechism of the Council of Trent.* Trans. John McHugh and Charles Callan. Rockford, IL: TAN Books, 1982.

Pius X, Pope. The Oath against Modernism *Sacrorum Antistitum* (1910).

Pius XI, Pope. Encyclical Letter *Divini Illius Magistri* (1929).

Pius XII, Pope. Apostolic Constitution *Munificentissimus Deus* (1950).

———. Encyclical Letter *Divino Afflante Spiritu* (1943).

————. Encyclical Letter *Humani Generis* (1950).

————. Encyclical Letter *Mystici Corporis* (1943).

Synod of Bishops XII Ordinary General Assembly. *Intrumentum Laboris* (2008).

Vatican Secretariat of State. *Regolamento Generale della Curia Romana* (1992).

Secondary Sources

Amato, Angelo. "The *Dominus Iesus* and the Other Religions." *Pro Dialogo: Pontificium Consilium pro Dialogo inter Religiones* 126 (2007): 230–250.

Aquinas, St. Thomas. *Disputed Questions on Truth*.

————. *Quodlibet IX*.

————. *Summa Theologiae*.

Augustine, St. *Against Faustus*.

————. *On Christian Doctrine*.

Beal, John P., et al., eds. *New Commentary on the Code of Canon Law*. New York: Paulist Press, 2000.

Beinert, Wolfgang. "Unfehlbarkeit." In *Lexicon für Theologie und Kirche*, 3rd ed, vol. 10. Ed. Walter Kasper. Freiburg im Breisgau: Herder, 1993–2001.

Bellarmine, St. Robert. *Controversies of the Christian Faith*. Trans. Kenneth Baker. Saddle River, NJ: Keep the Faith, 2016.

Bertone, Tarcisio. "Magisterial Documents and Public Dissent." *L'Osservatore Romano* (English), January 29, 1997.

Betti, Umberto. "Qualification théologique de la Constitution." In *L'Église de Vatican II*, vol. 2. Ed. Guilherme Baraúna. Paris: Cerf, 1967.

Billot, Louis. *Tractatus de Ecclesia Christi*. Rome: Giachetti, 1909.

Brown, Raymond E. *The Virginal Conception and Bodily Resurrection of Jesus*. New York: Paulist, 1973.

Butler, Cuthbert. *The Vatican Council.* London: Longmans and Green, 1930.

Cartechini, Sixtus. *De valore notarum theologicarum.* Rome, 1951.

Congar, Yves. "En guise de conclusion." In *L'Église de Vatican II,* vol. 3. Ed. Guilherme Baraúna. Paris: Cerf, 1967.

da Silva Tarouca, Carlos. *Institutiones historiae ecclesiasticae: Ecclesia in imperio Romano-Byzantino.* Rome: Gregorian University, 1933.

Dublanchy, Edmond. "Infaillibilité du Pape." In *Dictionnaire de théologie catholique.* Paris: Letouzey et Ané, 1927.

Dulles, Avery. "Catholicism and Capital Punishment." *First Things* (April 2001).

———. *Magisterium: Teacher and Guardian of the Faith.* Naples, FL: Sapientia Press, 2007.

Dunn, Matthew W. I. "The CDF's Declaration *Dominus Iesus* and Pope John Paul II." *Louvain Studies* 36 (2012): 46–75.

Fenton, Joseph C. "Infallibility in the Encyclicals." *American Ecclesiastical Review* 128 (1953): 177–98.

———. "*Sacrorum Antistitum* and the Background of the Oath Against Modernism." *American Ecclesiastical Review* 143 (1960): 239–260.

———. "The Doctrinal Authority of Papal Encyclicals." *American Ecclesiastical Review* 121 (1949): 136–50, 210–20.

Feser, Edward and Joseph Bessette. *By Man Shall His Blood Be Shed: A Catholic Defense of Capital Punishment.* San Francisco: Ignatius Press, 2017.

Fessler, Joseph. *Die wahre und die falsche Unfehlbarkeit der Päpste.* Vienna: Sartori, 1871.

Finnis, John. "Intentional Killing Is Always Wrong: The Development Initiated by Pius XII, Made by John Paul II, and Repeated by Francis." *Public Discourse,* August 22, 2018.

Franzelin, Johann Baptist. *Tractatus de divina traditione et scriptura.* Rome: Marietti, 1870.

Gaillardetz, Richard R. *Teaching with Authority: A Theology of the Magisterium of the Church.* Theology and Life, 41. Collegeville, MN: Liturgical, 1997.

Gómez-Iglesias, Valentín. "Naturaleza y origen de la confirmación *ex certa scientia.*" *Ius Canonicum* 25 (1985): 91–116.

Harrison, Brian W. "Paul VI on the Truth and Inerrancy of Sacred Scripture: Part B." *Living Tradition* 166 (2013).

———. "The *Ex Cathedra* Status of the Encyclical *Humanae Vitae.*" *Living Tradition* 43 (Sep.–Nov., 1992).

———. "Torture and Corporal Punishment as a Problem in Catholic Theology, Part II: The Witness of Tradition and Magisterium." *Living Tradition* 119 (Sep. 2005).

Hervé, Jean-Marie. *Manuale theologiae dogmaticae*, vol. 1. Paris: Berche & Pagis, 1935.

Huels, John M. "Interpreting an Instruction Approved *In Forma Specifica.*" *Studia Canonica* 32 (March 1998): 5–46.

Joy, John P. "*Cathedra Veritatis*: On the Extension of Papal Infallibility," STL thesis, International Theological Institute, 2012.

———. *On the Ordinary and Extraordinary Magisterium from Joseph Kleutgen to the Second Vatican Council.* Studia Oecumenica Friburgensia 84. Münster: Aschendorff, 2017.

Kleutgen, Joseph. *Die Theologie der Vorzeit verteidigt*, 2nd ed., vol. 1. Münster: Theissing, 1867.

Kwasniewski, Peter, ed. *Are Canonizations Infallible? Revisiting a Disputed Question.* Waterloo, ON: Arouca Press, 2021.

Lamont, John R. T. "The Authority of Canonizations." *Rorate Caeli*, Aug. 24, 2018.

Lio, Ermenegildo. *Humanae Vitae e Infallibilità: il Concilio, Paolo VI e Giovanni Paolo II.* Vatican City: Libreria Editrice Vaticana, 1986.

Lutheran-Roman Catholic Dialogue. "Teaching Authority and Infallibility in the Church: Common Statement." *Theological Studies* 40 (1979): 113–166.

Miller, Robert T. "Integralism and Catholic Doctrine." *Public Discourse*, July 15, 2018.

Morris, William. *Benedict, Me and the Cardinals Three: The Story of the Dismissal of Bishop Bill Morris by Pope Benedict XVI.* Adelaide: ATF Press, 2014.

Nau, Paul. "Le Magistère pontifical ordinaire au premier concile du Vatican." *Revue Thomiste* 62 (1962): 341–97.

Newman, St. John Henry. *A Letter Addressed to His Grace the Duke of Norfolk on Occasion of Mr. Gladstone's Recent Expostulation.* London: Pickering, 1875.

O'Regan, Emmett. "The Heretical Pope Fallacy: The Official *Relatio* of Vatican I on the Dogmatization of St. Bellarmine's 'Fourth Opinion'." *Vatican Insider*, December 11, 2017.

Ratzinger, Joseph. "Letter Concerning the CDF Reply Regarding *Ordinatio Sacerdotalis*." *L'Osservatore Romano* (English), November 19, 1995.

———. "The Limits of Church Authority." *L'Osservatore Romano* (English), June 29, 1994.

Salaverri, Joachim. *Tractatus de Ecclesia Christi.* Trans. Kenneth Baker. In *Sacrae Theologiae Summa*, vol. 1B. Saddle River, NJ: Keep the Faith, 2015.

Santogrossi, Ansgar. "Ordinatio Sacerdotalis: A definition ex cathedra." *Homiletic and Pastoral Review* (Feb. 1999): 7–14.

Schatz, Klaus. "Welche bisherigen päpstlichen Lehrentscheidungen sind '*ex cathedra*'? Historische und theologische

Überlegungen." In *Dogmengeschichte und katholische Theologie.* Ed. Werner Löser, Karl Lehmann, and Matthias Lutz-Bachmann. Würzburg: Echter, 1985.

Schmied, Augustin. "'Schleichende Infallibilisierung': Zur Diskussion um das kirchliche Lehramt." In *In Christus zum Leben befreit: Festschrift für Bernhard Häring.* Ed. Josef Römelt and Bruno Hidber. Freiburg: Herder, 1992.

Sullivan, Francis A. "The 'Secondary Object' of Infallibility." *Theological Studies* 54 (1993): 548–49.

———. "The Doctrinal Weight of *Evangelium vitae.*" *Theological Studies* 56 (1995): 560–565.

———. *Creative Fidelity: Weighing and Interpreting the Documents of the Magisterium.* Eugene: Wipf & Stock, 2003.

———. *Magisterium: Teaching Authority in the Catholic Church.* Eugene: Wipf & Stock, 2002.

Vacant, J.M.A. *Le magistère ordinaire de l'Eglise et ses organes.* Paris: Delhomme et Briguet, 1887).

Valente, Gianni. Interview with Cardinal Georges Cottier. "Paul VI, Maritain and the Faith of the Apostles." *30 Days* 4 (2008).

Walford, Stephen. "The Magisterium of Pope Francis: His Predecessors Come to His Defense." *Vatican Insider*, February 7, 2017.

Index of Topics

Index of Names